The Rider's Balance

SYLVIA LOCH

The Rider's Balance

Understanding the
weight aids
in pictures

KENILWORTH PRESS

*The art of putting weight into the stirrups is the subtlest
of all the aids; the rider's legs then serve as counterweights
to straighten the haunches and to hold the horse straight...*

Sieur François Robichon de la Guérinière (1733)

DEDICATION

This book is dedicated to Prazer – my Lusitano hotblood stallion – bred by the Oliveira e Sousa Stud in Portugal, 1996.

He was bought as a youngster by Richard and Melanie James who imported him to England. Subsequently, Prazer came to my stables in Scotland for schooling and despite my move south at a later date, has never left my side!

I will be forever grateful to the James's not only for entrusting him into my care, but furthermore allowing me to buy and keep him when they had to relocate to New Zealand.

Prazer has turned into the most amazing, kind and generous horse I have ever had the privilege to own – and there have been many – in the six decades to date.

Throughout the years, he has touched and changed the lives of many people. At 22 years old, he is still full of fire and vigour for his Mum, yet the moment a student is in the saddle, all is calm again. He really is the horse of a lifetime – heaven-sent I believe.

Copyright © 2018 Sylvia Loch

First published in the UK in 2018
by Kenilworth Press, an imprint of Quiller Publishing Ltd

Distributed in the USA by Trafalgar Square Books,
www.HorseandRiderBooks.com

British Library Cataloguing-in-Publication Data
A catalogue record for this book is available from the
British Library

ISBN 978 1 91001 634 3

Design by Guy Callaby

Printed in Malaysia

Kenilworth Press
An imprint of Quiller Publishing Ltd
Wykey House, Wykey, Shrewsbury SY4 1JA
Tel: 01939 261616
Email: info@quillerbooks.com
Website: www.quillerpublishing.com

Contents

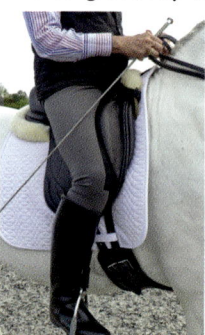

Foreword

Most serious dressage riders will be familiar with the teachings of Sylvia Loch, studied and practised over her many years devoted to horses.

For my part, I first discovered her in *Horse & Rider* magazine and she always explained things very clearly so that one could take on board even quite complicated instructions. She made the reader feel as though they could accomplish these movements and exercises for themselves – the description of the aids being so crystal clear. It seemed all was possible with one's horse or pony, even although some of the work was surprisingly advanced.

I always liked the idea of *The Classical Seat*, Sylvia's first book – and how important it was to sit tall and make things easier for the horse underneath. Throughout my career in dressage, this has been one of the most important factors of my own work. How can a horse be balanced if his rider is not balanced too?

I also like the idea of elegance that the classical work brings to the relationship. So many riders seem unaware that a central, upright position and quiet, discreet aids will work for their horse so much better than moving about and doing too much – as is too often seen.

Sylvia's explanation of the weight aids is something which all serious riders and trainers should aspire to understand and take on board. Not enough is written about 'feel' and often this is difficult to put into words. Now, the excellent explanations in this book – much helped by the photographs – should leave us in no doubt.

The Rider's Balance is very clearly written and will help both riders and trainers understand better exactly what their horse needs to feel from them. My mentor and trainer, Carl Hester, has always spoken to me about the importance of a good seat and every aspect of balance. With his encouragement and example, it is something I work on every single day.

For this reason, the advice offered in Sylvia's amazing new book should really help all horses and their riders. Only by understanding how our posture and weight impacts on the horse can we develop a meaningful sense of communication and partnership. This is so important if we are to move on and take ourselves and our horse to a higher plane.

Charlotte Dujardin CBE

About Sylvia –
A Special Connection

Tommy – the very first pony of my own.

Right *Trojan was deemed 'unrideable and dangerous' when he came to me when we were both aged ten; he eventually turned into a 'butter wouldn't melt' pony.*

My whole life from the age of five upwards has been dominated by horses. First, the Clydesdales, massive working horses on my father's farm in Scotland; second the first pony, gymkhanas, jumping and Pony Club; third, a never-forgotten-trip to Badminton which opened my eyes to what might be ... and fourth, hacking and hunting across wild, glorious country. It was a moment of real pride when, at the age of 16, I was offered Mercury, our Master's beautiful but highly sensitive Thoroughbred mare – whom he confessed he couldn't handle at all. She was tall, grey and beautiful; she galloped like the wind, jumped like a stag, yet never scared me at all. I loved her.

Bizarre as it may sound, I began to teach riding quite seriously aged just fifteen. Not only other children, but their parents too. My father and mother supported me, probably relieved I hadn't yet got into boys and was doing something close to my heart. In the summer I organised summer camps – based on what I had learned at Girl Guides – and Pony Club. It was much more challenging being the instructor, rather than the instructed – but I loved it. I followed the teachings and ethos of the *British Manual of Horsemanship* and faithfully passed on these traditional, cavalry-based methods to the children in my care.

Starting with two rescue ponies whom I had bought and schooled on, the two became four and by the time I was eighteen, we had ten. A spell in London took me away from horses, but they were always part of my soul.

In addition to the many hours spent in the saddle, schooling and teaching from an early age, I also learned a lot by reading. Gradually, even the most tricky and obstinate of mounts turned into nice schoolmasters for my young charges. I believe it all worked because I kept the work consistent, encouraged and rewarded and can truthfully say, never raised my voice or lost my temper. Unfortunately, I have a terrible allergy to horses which – without exaggeration –

almost killed me a couple of times. I suffered with severe asthma, bronchitis, pneumonia – and there were a number of hospital visits. The worst scenario was to happen in Portugal in the early 1970s. The hospital ward – if you could call it that – happened to be next door to an asylum. There was a point where an inmate came wandering in and tried to disconnect my oxygen. An anxious moment ... but fortunately I survived.

I had tried, for a while, to give up on horses. Aged 21, I became director's secretary in the whisky industry, which was both serious and fun. Later, I moved to publishing, then unexpectedly, aged just 23 to discotheques! A year at sea running the first proper disco on an enormous passenger liner took me round the world and not a sneeze in sight. Cruising round the Mediterranean, then down into North Africa, the Canaries and Madeira was incredible. The old European city ports were stunning, but when we crossed the Equator and sailed down to South Africa and South America that can only be described as dreams come true.

Trigger – He may have been plain but he was the most brilliant jumper and gymkhana pony anyone could have wished for. I won more rosettes with Trigger than any other horse/pony.

Back on terra firma I was content for a while, but Fate being what it is, I was pulled back to riding in the most unexpected way. I was offered a job in Portugal – and who could have foreseen that I would meet and marry one of the greatest horsemen in the world – Lord Henry Loch. Quite out of the blue, I was thrown back into an equestrian world that many would give their eye teeth for.

The rest is history, ten years in Portugal, transporting a whole school of horses from our Algarve home to Suffolk, building an equestrian centre which practically bankrupted us and finding ourselves at the butt end of the English establishment – we suffered highs and lows. In those days, the late 1970s, people didn't 'do' classical dressage. In competition it was the harsher German way that found popularity with the judges and if you rode with a softer rein, you were accused of riding behind the bit. We were out in the cold, but our pupils loved us and our school grew ... slowly but surely.

Henry Loch was an ex-cavalry commander. If any man loved and understood horses it was him. People were mesmerised watching his every move, the way in which he looked a horse in the eye, touched them, handled them. He always used the same low, calming voice with each – stallion or mare: 'Hello, old thing ...' and they knew immediately he was their friend. He was magnetic. Once in the saddle, he was incredibly calm – mesmeric – rode like a Roman emperor. He had hands of silk and

My late husband Henry Loch. Always in breeches.

We built the most stunning yard together, not knowing we would only have three years to enjoy it.

could transform a difficult horse in minutes. As a former Royal Hussar, much of his understanding came from his early training as a young cavalry officer combined with a passion for the old classic books. I doubt I've ever seen anyone look so at one with the horse. Everything was quiet, effortless.

It was the same on the ground. Henry was a man of very few words. You learned more by watching him than by what he had to say, as he was dyslexic and could struggle. He was also an alcoholic – I knew him both in and out of the grip of addiction – and I know the horses helped us both to deal with it. They never judged; they seemed to understand; they were our friends. Henry's last three years on this earth were alcohol-free and he was proud of it. We all were.

After the Portuguese Revolution in 1975, we had struggled on with overseas riders flying out to enjoy our horses and the sunshine, but it was a difficult time for all. We had to buy in water from the local town as we were not yet on the mains, electricity was by generator, hay was almost impossible to buy and much else besides. Our dressage courses were going well, but there were only two Lusitanos in the UK at the time and our students were putting pressure on us to transfer our entire school of mainly High School stallions and mares to England. It made sense to return to the family home in Suffolk.

Classical riding was just in its infancy in the UK, and the School of Lightness almost unheard of. One of our first great supporters at our newly built yard was Lucinda Green – or Prior-Palmer as she was known then. She wrote a glowing report of our methods in *Riding* magazine and from then on, the telephone never stopped ringing. Henry was on the map, the Lusitanos, too.

When Henry died quite suddenly in 1982, just after the birth of our daughter, it might have all come to an end. But the horses had other ideas,

Peacock and me outside our indoor school in Suffolk.

and so had I. We had not come all this way for nothing and amongst his coterie of students, he had left a great legacy. 'Tell them!', he used to say to me. 'Tell them how horses like to be ridden. Go on with the work'

From then on, I took Henry's ethos forward and I was teaching almost every day. Over the years that followed, I covered the length and breadth of the UK and gave clinics in the US, New Zealand, South Africa, Canada and Australia as well as mainland Europe, but people wanted more. When, finally, I launched the Classical Riding Club in 1995, it was my way of preserving all that Henry had taught me. We may have been a few years ahead of our time, but by the year 2000 the CRC – as it came to be known – had taken off, with members all over the world.

By this time, I was writing almost as much as I was teaching. My book *The Royal Horse of Europe* (1986) was to take me to Buckingham Palace at the time of the Portuguese Presidential visit and my first teaching book *The Classical Seat* (1988) had become a bestseller although it had caused much controversy at the time. But the book that really made a difference was *The Classical Rider* (1990). This was about the philosophy of riding as well as the history and practicalities and more and more people were looking for a kinder, more embracing and holistic form of instruction. The old push, pull and kick-on mentality that had turned me off so much in my younger days was starting to fade. People wanted better.

I was very lucky during my years of training and writing, to meet some extraordinary authorities from the world of dressage. In Portugal, I had known the 'greats' including, of course, Mestre Nuno Oliveira, with whom I spent a week as we discussed his life and philosophy for a biography. Sadly,

My love affair with dressage started in Portugal.

this never came to fruition as he died very suddenly in Australia a few months later. The legacy of his books has helped make up for this and I never tire of returning to his first and truly great book – *Reflections on Equestrian Art*. Only an artist could have written this, and only someone who understood every action and attitude of horses both young and old.

A friendship, that transported me back into history and led to my fascination with the Spanish Riding School of Vienna and the Austro-Hungarian Empire, was formed with Madame Eva Podhajsky. As the widow of the great Colonel Alois Podhajsky (who, with General Patton, had saved the Lipizzaners from a dreadful fate during the Second World War), Eva came to stay in our home in England on two different occasions. She much encouraged me, even being so good as to watch me teach and then to write the Foreword of *The Classical Rider*.

Through Eva, I became friendly with General Kurt Albrecht, another figurehead and director of The Spanish Riding School who followed after Colonel Handler. Soon afterwards, I got to know Oberbereiter Hans Riegler, who generously agreed to be our speaker at Wembley when I ran a special conference for the CRC after the School's performance at Birmingham. Later, through the Training the Teachers of Tomorrow Trust, I was to take lessons from former Chief Rider Arthur Kottas, a very special person. The thing I loved about Arthur's lessons was not so much his sharp eye and cutting impatience with humans, but the fact all horses adore him. They still do today – 25 years on! Not dissimilar to Henry, his love of the horse shines out during his lessons and this, I have come to discover, is a rare thing. Horses know when they are loved and they respond in a very different and positive way.

In France, another great lover of the horse was a special man called Colonel Tatton. He was father of a wise, elegant lady I had become close to through diplomatic circles. When his daughter Lady Brigitte Scott-Fox died recently, she left me a fantastic collection of equestrian books. Then there were the Henriquets. Michel, who was an ardent admirer and friend of Nuno Oliveira, had invited me to stay at the home he shared with Catherine – soon to be his wife – just outside Versailles. He was a hard taskmaster. Quite rightly, he was very picky with students and I have to confess that, during my time with them, I was glad I was there to write – not to take lessons!

I first met the highly academic French trainer, Colonel Christian Carde when I went to give a clinic at Saumur in the early 2000s. Later, he generously came to the UK to participate at the Classical Riding Club's (CRC) Twenty-first Anniversary Dressage Convention in 2016. The French School, even in recent times, has always been based on the teachings of the eighteenth-century Master Sieur de La Guérinière. Sadly, however, the Henriquets and Cardes of this world are fast disappearing. Today, a more modern approach is eclipsing the old classical ways in France, with a number of 'new methods' being taught which, for me, are at odds with the classical ethos.

One more person I must mention as a classical purist was the late Dr Reiner Klimke. He was one of the few riders of world renown to excel

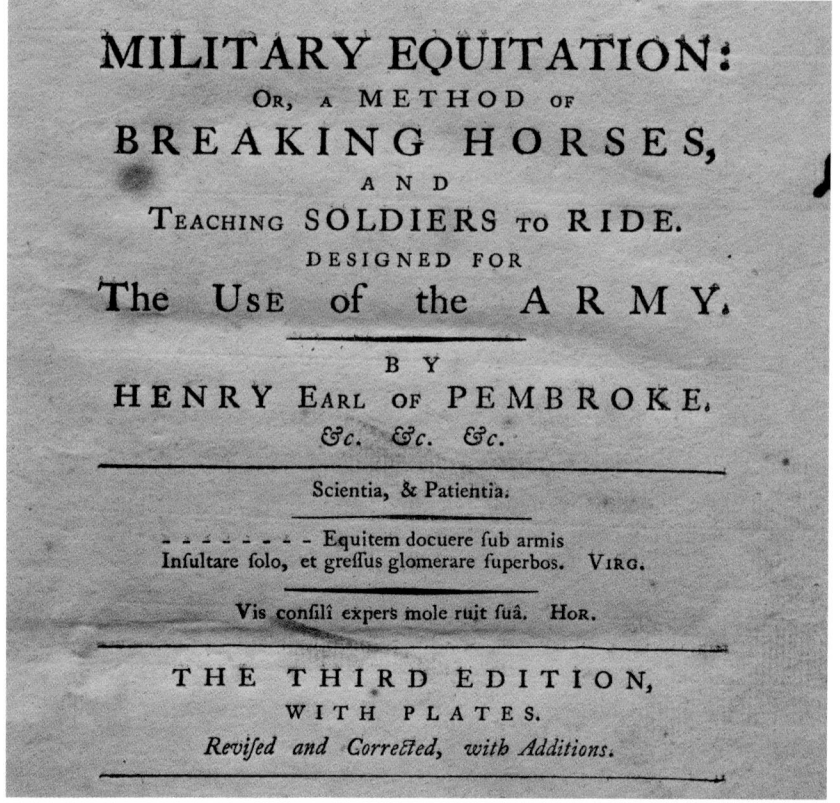

I started writing equestrian books in 1975 and haven't really stopped. Old books like these have inspired me and taught me so much. My library is priceless to me.

at top-level competition work without in any way compromising his virtuosity and passion for classical riding. Flatteringly, he always embraced me like a long-lost friend when we met up at international events. On one occasion at Equitana in Kentucky, he was good enough to sit with me and share his opinion of the ensuing dressage exhibition. Together, we watched several Grand Prix tests one long afternoon and his observations on both competitors and their judges were fascinating. His love of the horse shone out of him – and I was struck, not for the first time, how few trainers exude this rather necessary quality.

Once trained, I truly believe horses will give you everything if you love them. But what good is love if there is no understanding? The former is

Prazer – My horse of a lifetime. He has also helped change the life of so many of my students.

deep within the psyche; the latter has to be learned and acquired. This may take years – for many, a lifetime.

Once the tools are in place and the horse understands us as well as our understanding him, it is all about trust – allowing, wanting the best for him and believing in it. Discipline and gentle correction are important – but the latter should never be a punishment. It just means we do it again, and again – until we get there. This may take five minutes or five months.

Giving a horse the benefit of the doubt can be hard. Everyone is looking for perfection, but this is not realistic. Everything needs to be done step by step and the whole ethos of schooling and training concerns doing things incrementally and with great patience. It depends on the aptitude of the horse and – what is too often forgotten – our own aptitude. And every time there is an improvement, we reward. How can a horse learn without confirmation and approbation too?

When I work with a student, I note a big difference between those who look their horse in the eye – and those who don't. Focus is all, not just on the job in hand but from within. It connects us, from the heart and soul, and horses, being such sentient creatures, feel it. Those who are loved will naturally give more back. In my fifty-odd years of teaching, I have seen this confirmed again and again.

Riding is such a personal thing I am constantly amazed that every rider does not feel a sense of wonder every time they look at their horse. Think about it! Isn't it something of a miracle that your horse lets you place your foot in the stirrup and mount up in the first place? As for carrying you and doing all the amazing things he does ... we absolutely owe it to him – never to stop learning. ■

Introduction

When my last book *The Balanced Horse* was published, I said at the time there wouldn't be another book. I thought I had said it all. Today, however, I take that back. There is always something more to learn, something more to give out, and the longer one lives the more one's empathy grows. I realise that now, in my seventies, I know more about the riding of horses than I did at sixty and more still than I did in my fifties. And I am still riding, of course, so I feel and learn every day – and that is invaluable in the training of others.

A good trainer really cares about the horses that come before them for schooling, and there are always fresh insights. No horse is the same, no rider either, and each and every combination is different. It is for that reason I felt compelled to write *The Rider's Balance*. We may have the best, most athletic and willing horse in the world, but if our aids are not clear and our understanding is lacking, we can compromise him to the extent of losing all his natural talent and willingness to please. I have seen too many horses around me to whom this has happened and there are several out there who have just 'given up'.

To all my students, Prazer is generous beyond belief and incredibly patient.

Instead, I want to see all riders improve their horses. Those who are naturally athletic will go further – even reaching giddy heights. Those who are average should be greatly improved and made happy. But without good riding technique none of this is possible.

It is largely because of the innate goodness of horses that I first felt driven to teach and write about them. They truly are friends to humankind and have served us selflessly over generations and centuries. Watching *The Charge of the Light Brigade* on television only a few weeks ago – years after it was first released – I found tears pouring down my face. Horses thundering into battle as gallantly and trustingly as they would gallop out with the hunt, or along the beach ... and nothing spared.

What saddens (and at times angers) me is that all too often people treat horses with ignorance and do not take the trouble to learn to ride them as they themselves would like to be ridden. They also fail to sense the huge intelligence and generosity of horses. How many times do you hear the words ... 'stupid horse'? No, horses are not stupid – it is we who are stupid by failing them through our own ignorance.

I find it amazing that we can train horses to perform movements that may compromise their own balance, yet they do it willingly and incredibly accurately at the slightest command from us. They bow to our superiority in the natural pecking order. Often, the smallest aid will achieve a result. Horses clearly have amazing memories too. It is not unusual to sit on a horse who may not have performed dressage movements for years, yet the moment the correct aids are applied, they are back into the swing of things and extraordinary reactions and sequences are offered at 'the touch of a button'.

I was once asked 'Why do you have such old horses?' I answered that surely it was obvious. Having bought them as youngsters, I have schooled them in such a way that they last! Surely, it is no coincidence that horses who are still being ridden in their twenties generally belong to people who have taken the trouble to learn a methodology and a way of riding that is best for the horse. My late husband Henry Loch used to say 'My horse is my

Prazer adores being used as a schoolmaster and is a great inspiration to all my students. I am sure he knows he is appreciated and still, at 22 years of age, offers beautiful movements.

visiting card.' In other words, you will know me by my horse.

Generally, correct, logical riding is referred to as classical riding ... but classical riding is not just a fancy term for showing off on a horse. It should mean that the horse is ridden from start to finish through proven and tested methods that work with both his body and his mind. I don't believe it is just repetition that allows a horse to offer all the lovely movements we see in dressage with riders like Charlotte Dujardin and Carl Hester. I know it is more than this. It is obvious to anyone who has an eye for a horse that the horse will give back what he can when he is ridden correctly and empathetically. They offer far more through their innate sense of pride and joy and this is not always recognised.

So next time you school your horse, expect nothing for granted. Instead, dwell on how you feel to him through the saddle. Ride your horse as you would like to be ridden. He deserves nothing less.

Anyone interested in dressage and who watches today's top Olympic echelon will acknowledge there is very little difference in the riding position of most competitors. Times have changed from the days when people talked about the German seat, the English seat and so on. Nowadays, there is very little difference.

Above *I found Prazer in Oxfordshire – newly imported from Portugal in 2003. After two years at my home in Scotland, he came back with me to Portugal where I was running my clinics near Lisbon. Back in the UK for the past decade, we are never far apart.*

Right *The Spanish Riding School has been a great influence on my life and I was lucky enough to spend time with Madame Podhajsky in Vienna.*

The Classical Riding Club's 21st Anniversary Event attracted over 350 attendees and Prazer enjoyed himself as much as anyone.

More marked, perhaps, is the contrast in style between the riders of the Spanish Riding School of Vienna, the Portuguese School of Equestrian Art and the Andalusian School, and those of normal riding schools throughout the world. This is a great pity and there is no reason at all why people should not aspire to riding with the grace, poise and knowledge that are generally the preserve of the élite.

I have always encouraged all my students to read the classical books, ride well-schooled horses whenever possible and strive to emulate both the posture and the aids of those riders we look up to. It is for all riders that this book is written. Indeed, there is no reason at all why every riding student should not aspire to riding correctly – generally known as classical riding.

This is my eighth equestrian book. I have previously written at great length on the seat, the aids, how to school for all the various dressage movements from the most basic to the more advanced, as well as a special book on my philosophy. This book is rather different. I wanted to produce something rather simple and more visual – something that can be understood in an instant – not so much by reading, but by looking.

Observation is a great gift to which we are all privy. The thing you have to know is what you are looking for. I could show one person a picture of my horse and they might say 'lovely horse'. I might show another to an experienced rider, and they could say 'too much this' or 'too much that' and they might be right. Here, photographs are telling lots of stories: explaining to the reader why and how something is right and just as importantly, when something is wrong. The captions will help as well.

The main object of this book is about discerning what needs to be done and what shouldn't be done. You may not always notice the differences because the aids may (or may not) be very subtle. One cannot always see from a photograph exactly how a stirrup is weighted, a seatbone moved forward or how the seatbones affect the horse's back, but it's amazing how one can get the gist. A more advanced rider with a practised eye will obviously be quicker to spot the difference.

Look for the horse's expression – his ears and eyes being a great giveaway – look for the way in which he carries himself, where his hind legs are placed and his general outline: is it softly arched or artificially tensed? In this book we have advanced horses and we have novice horses. We have different breeds and different riders. Every combination is different, but we are all bound and governed by the same laws of gravity, animal and human.

To help, I have, where possible, illustrated through arrows on the drawings by Maggie Raynor exactly where the rider's weight or pressure aid is being utilised. There may be one or two, even several different aids going on, but all must complement each other and it is the whole

Sylvia put on The Classical Dressage Seminar in 2014 at Ladykirk in Scotland, which attracted riders of all disciplines.

effect that matters. Horses generally respond – and when they do, they do not lie!

To make this book more interesting and relevant to all horses and riders, I have tried – as much as possible – to use horses of different types and sizes, and both horses and riders of different levels and experience. There is no such thing in my opinion as a perfect horse or indeed the perfect rider ... but most horses will try their heart out for you. The way you use your weight is of utmost importance to each and every horse. Generally, he wants to be able to carry you, he will almost invariably 'pick you up' if you get it wrong and by using these methods your partnership should be greatly enhanced. I hope this book will encourage and inspire you even more.

By using the correct weight aids I believe you can make your relationship with your horse even better. He won't have read this book, but once you start to think about where you are in space and use the aids described gently and logically, your horse will respond to the feeling you impart. Once he is encouraged and helped to move into your balance, he will understand what you want in the most surprising and often rewarding way. I wish you both luck! ■

I have never felt quite such a connection as I do with this horse.

23

1 Mindfulness
Riding in Your Head

For me, focus and connection is everything in the schooling of every horse in my care. Whatever we ask of our horse – simple or demanding – he deserves one hundred per cent of our concentration.

For many, it can be challenging to describe what we feel and how we feel when schooling a horse or training a student to ride their horse better. Some will talk of one hundred per cent concentration, others may focus on a particular goal, yet others may speak of a blank canvas. They wait for something to present itself.

We are all different. For my part, I feel I move onto a different plane and am wholly committed to the process in hand, for however long it lasts. I am sure I am not alone in this. Mindfulness is the modern word for describing what we are going through. It covers empathy, involvement and total concentration.

Basically, working one to one with another living being – in this case, the horse – you are fully attending mentally to the matter in hand, as it is happening, and as it unfolds. Quite simply, it draws you into another world – to quote from the web – 'the space we are moving through'. In other words, it involves total absorption of both mind and body.

The following summation from the internet is pretty accurate: 'Mindfulness is the basic human ability to be fully present, aware of where we are and what we're doing, and not overly reactive or overwhelmed by what's going on around us.'

I believe this is what all riders should aim for – especially in the dressage arena or school. For that period of time in which we are working with our horse, we need to remember that this is another sensitive living being, whose every move is subject to our balance and our body. If we care about him and want the work to be accurate and pleasurable, it behoves us to give him the whole of our attention and understanding. That involves mindfulness.

For example, there is all the difference in the world between riding a horse and going for a bike ride. In the latter, it would be quite normal and natural not to be mindful. Instead, we might have several different

As shown here, we complement the horse's balance by looking through his ears. Our head weighs about 14 pounds, so any deviation will spoil the picture.

We owe it to the horse to sit in perfect balance. Here, the rein becomes superfluous other than to maintain a light contact.

Right *Even on the unschooled horse, the tiniest 'ask' with the fingers will elicit a response. Horses thrive on small aids.*

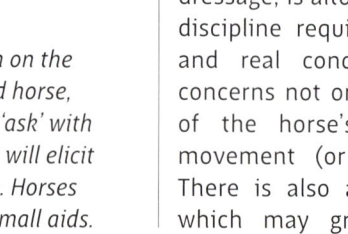

thoughts floating through our head at once without interfering with our ability to cycle. After all, we can hardly commune with a pair of handlebars and pedals in the same way as communicating through the reins, seat and stirrups to a living animal.

I may be wrong, but generally in cycling or indeed driving a car to and from the yard every day, I can think of a myriad of other things without losing concentration on the road and the traffic. You may be able to cope with everything from remembering your shopping list to what you need to say to your partner, business colleague or best friend. Even mentally preparing a special speech should not deter you from the task in hand. And you may have the added distraction of the radio, but you can cope with that too.

Equitation, and particularly dressage, is altogether different. The discipline requires both sensitivity and real concentration, since it concerns not only every movement of the horse's body, but every movement (or aid) of our own. There is also an artistic element, which may greatly enhance our

approach – not just to the horse but to the subject as a whole. Many of the signals we give out may be involuntary, but a thoughtful rider will seek to identify when *not* to do something, as well as what and when to *do*. Timing and balance are of the utmost importance – no one can entirely teach us those. They come with experience and learning through feel, and the greatest reward of all is when the horse tells us we have got it right.

Therefore, to improve on what comes logically – as well as naturally – relies largely on developing self-knowledge. In this way, and over time, we develop a greater awareness and control over our whole body – so that we can in turn aid the horse to control his.

When it comes to teaching, mindfulness will again play an all-consuming part. Not only does the trainer become absorbed in the horse, they also have the rider to 'take on board'. Both good riders and good trainers will develop an inbuilt sense of being in the moment and that should continue for as long as they are schooling or teaching. In my own experience, the fact that someone has entered the gallery or is watching our lesson from the side will generally pass me by. An aeroplane high overhead will tend to be ignored – even 'noises off' become an irrelevance.

In the giving of the rein, the mare acknowledges her freedom to stretch.

It is good for horse and rider to stand still in the middle of training. Time to reflect and take stock.

I become so absorbed in the process – the whole partnership of horse and rider – that everything else is extraneous.

This is an altogether different scenario from what we may feel when entering the stable, seeing a horse being shod, studying horses in the paddock or watching a dressage test. Because we love horses, of course we will be interested in all of these aspects – observant and often admiring – but this is not necessarily being mindful.

When I am teaching, everything changes – I no longer notice things that are going on around us – instead the horses 'suck me in' and it is as though time has stood still. I am now totally and utterly absorbed into their world. I can almost feel what they are feeling – which can be disturbing when seeing and sensing bad mistakes being made. I rush to try to correct such things, but of course that doesn't always work right away.

Right *My first priority when teaching is to connect with both the horse and rider.*

This may sound shocking, but there have been moments of tragedy in my life where I have found myself ignoring the unfolding distress, simply because I have been with my horses. It is not about not caring, or having a hard heart – quite the reverse. Despite probably being in trauma, because our focus is entirely on the horse, or a particular partnership, there is a temporary removal from the source of the trauma. This has happened to me, and in both cases involved the sudden death of someone very dear and very close.

The point being, as long as I was with my horses and within the familiar confines of my school, I was in a safe place. You could say I was transported to a different world. I was in the moment – feeling through my rider, or my stallion underneath – noting, as usual, what needed to be done. And it was very healing. For that one hour, I was taken out of my grief and into the present world of that horse and that rider.

Mindfulness is not *necessarily* a release. We all 'live in our head' and that brings with it many responsibilities. We are all different, but a good rider or a good trainer will actually feel the balance of the horse, the mood of the horse, his strengths and his weaknesses, within their soul. This gift is developed with time – earned through practice and acute observation.

Of course, our eyes are all-important. I have this 'thing' about the rider's head position. If the rider is not looking through the horse's ears – at all times – and in all the movements – connection is lost. Horses know when you are looking with them. You are not fixated on their ears or any part of the neck in front of you, but you are with them by softly focusing in exactly the same way as they themselves. The two of you are together.

Moving onto the track, both horse and rider should be flexed into the direction of travel.

I do a lot of riding in my head. This may sound rather fanciful, but it is true. Our thoughts, our brain, our eyes, our focus are all controlled by and through our head. For me it is inconceivable not to be 'joined up' with the horse in this way. I truly believe every horse – even the difficult ones – will feel where our gaze is and will make the choice whether or not to connect with us because of it.

Watching other riders, I see the sensitive ones operating in the same way. Every small movement required of the horse is mirrored by their own body and, in particular, through their head position. They may not necessarily be the world's greatest riders, but it is a huge bonus when the rider has the empathy to deport themselves in this way.

Never forget that our eyes and our head position affect everything we do. When we are in harmony with our own bodies, when we are thinking about what we are doing, and when we ride with our mind as well as physically, the results will be plain to see. Mindfulness will help us to help ourselves and to help the horse. In or out of the saddle, we feel it – in our bones, in our souls. For as long as it lasts – two minutes, ten minutes, an hour – we are committed to that partnership. The minutes may tick by, but time makes no difference.

Always focus, go with the flow and the balance of the movement. Allow gravity to do its job.

Teaching dressage can be a very intimate experience. Years and years of practice is invaluable and body language tells us so much. The horse's ears and expression are great giveaways. But there's more to it than that. The connection through the horse's eye to the trainer on the ground can be compelling. It can reveal how he wants to be ridden, how the smallest change will make a difference and how he depends on us to show the rider exactly what is required.

It is often more a matter of freeing him up rather than telling him to do more. I am shocked how many riders hang onto the rein when the trainer has drawn them into the centre to stop and explain something. Why not give the rein for those few precious seconds? In the army, it would be 'stand at ease'. Why not the same for the horse?

I have been at many training sessions either as a bystander or member of the audience, and whilst some sessions have been inspirational, others have been painful. Mindfulness and empathy can make it very hard not to interfere. As most of us know, not every trainer will possess the same qualities. Some treat the horse like a machine. The demeanour of each and every horse gives away so much, but we need the eyes to see beyond and we need the knowledge in our head, to make real progress.

The stretch on the long rein is as important to the development of the horse's topline as is the more collected work. It refreshes both horse and rider.

At the end of the day, all we can do is make more people aware of those special signals that horses and other animals give out. It's important to talk about it. Empathy and working with two live beings bear heavy responsibilities. As riders or instructors, we are not just there to command. Far from it − we are there to help. And the rewards must be obvious; horses know when you are on their side and will give back such a lot.

Without the theory of riding it is very hard to improve either the student or the horse. We can see the mistakes, but we need the knowledge and the empathy to sort out the problems. To be there for the horse as well as the rider is very important. It is a huge privilege to teach dressage and, while life may be made easier with a talented rider, it is often more rewarding to bring about real improvement − even if it is never going to be perfect.

When I say goodbye at the end of another lesson, the hardest questions are, 'Despite the best teaching in the world, is the rider capable of taking it forward? Will riding become a better experience for both rider and horse?' The rider will certainly have to learn to be mindful for this to be so. ∎

2 The Weight Aids
Feeling, Understanding and Employing Them

After fifty years of teaching, one of the most important pieces of advice I would give to a young rider is this. Sit up! Think where you want to go and allow it to happen. Whatever his breed, type, personality or size — be a leader to your horse.

Beginner riders often have a better natural posture than the more experienced. It feels right to think up; generally the horse will respond in kind.

Clearly, in order to do this, it is necessary to be pro-active and this is where our understanding of posture and weight becomes so important. Much is talked about the horse being in balance, but if the rider is not equally in balance with their own body, how can the horse be expected to cope? Only by understanding the effects of our position and how and where pressure should be directed will we be able to train a horse correctly and with dignity.

Dressage demands both collection and engagement. The gymnastic exercises that follow are all designed to strengthen the horse behind and lighten the forehand.

In dressage training, the main objective of the schooling exercises is to teach the horse to rebalance and transfer his weight to the hind end. However, if we ourselves are unable to manage our weight and have no understanding how each aid we apply impacts on the horse's balance, we will both be left struggling.

So we have two issues to consider:

● The horse's weight.

● Our own weight.

Weight back

Training the horse to shift his weight back can only be done progressively and my previous book *The Balanced Horse* deals in great detail with the schooling process.

Below *The more we ask the horse to bend and stretch, the more he will learn to step under our weight, but this takes time. The inside leg deepens at the girth – while the rider's outside shoulder moves round in harmony with that of the horse.*

Unfortunately, a young horse will nearly always tend to lean on the forehand to escape the burdensome task of carrying the rider – which is all very natural. We should not get frustrated by this but, right from the beginning, we have a chance to make a real difference.

By sitting up and asking with the leg at the girth for the horse to lift through the forehand, the horse's own posture can be immediately improved, especially in the rising trot. Hacking out lends itself to plenty of upward and downward transitions – all of which should be done with a light seat at the beginning of training – our weight basically borne by the stirrups.

Riding out to the corner requires bend and balance. Keep the inside leg at the girth for flexion, but try gently weighting the outside stirrup to take the horse out.

In the school, circles and turns will work the horse's body each way and generally it is better to start these in walk before progressing to trot – although much depends on the horse's temperament. Bend to the inside and stretch to the outside is the name of the game. With plenty of changes of rein and straight lines in between, we will even up the horse's natural crookedness. In this way, we gradually teach the horse to transfer weight from the forehand to the hind end as well as building up muscle tone.

Always ride out to the track and into your corners and your horse will gradually learn to step more under himself. Over time, this teaches him to bend his hocks and carry more weight behind. Instead of leaning on the hand, he will start to take responsibility for his own balance, straighten out and feel easier and lighter on the bit.

Once the horse's weight is brought back, we can then enjoy a horse who is attentive, supple and strong through the back as well as fully engaged behind. Horses trained correctly in this way will tend to last well into their late teens and twenties, provided we treat them with respect. They are less like to have joint problems and the muscling over the neck, back and quarters will look rounded and healthy.

Managing our own weight

What has become more and more obvious to me in recent years is that many riders know all this but many are not by any means well-versed in the aids, which would enable them to bring about a suitable programme of work.

Too many treat the young horse as though he were strong and mature from day one, and many a horse has been ruined by a thoughtless rider who has little conception of how they impinge on the horse's back.

This brings us to an understanding of how our weight can either make life tolerable or harder for both horse and rider. Too many riders seem to battle to train their horse, getting off exhausted at the end of a schooling session. Instead, by learning to channel their weight correctly, they can discover a much easier way forward.

Most showjumpers or event riders are all too aware of how important it is to adjust their weight as they ride their horse into a fence. To come in straight, a little more pressure here – a little more weight into this or that stirrup – a slight tilt of the body to right or left, even the direction in which they are looking, are all essential aids. Often, these are performed automatically.

What are less talked about are the weight aids that we should be using in dressage. For many dressage riders, the very mention of this term may cause surprise or concern. Yet, most of it is common sense.

In equitation the term 'weight aid' helps us to understand the effect of harnessing or allowing gravity to act on our bodies to improve the balance of our horse. This may be applied through our seat or our feet or, more often, both. The outcome should be to achieve a harmonious partnership whereby horse and rider appear to move as one.

For example, on our own two feet, downward pressure is applied every time we move forward. Our weight goes straight down into the ground. We step into the right foot and, whether we are conscious of it or not, we experience the downward pull of gravity. A moment later, we step into the left foot and the result is the same. In fact, there will be a weight shift

Weighting the stirrups is very normal in jumping; it should not be forgotten in all disciplines.

Right *We do not have to push against the ground, or indeed the stirrup – gravity should take our weight down for us.*

Walking

Jogging/Running

Below left *Sitting tall but weighting the inside seatbone invites the horse to move and bend left around the rider's inside leg.*

Below right *On the bigger circle, the rider maintains the inside leg at the girth position, but the weight aid to the inside (right) will be less noticeable.*

in everything we do. This includes standing, walking, running, skipping or dancing. It also includes riding.

Just like us, the horse is subject to the effects of gravity and has to use and respond to them if he is to move and function easily. There is the added issue of the rider's weight influencing the horse's. If he were to resist this, there would be no partnership. Without working together, both he and we might be quite unstable. It is up to us therefore to use our aids judiciously.

As well as downward pressure – weight down – there is sideways pressure whereby we can move the horse away or bring him in towards us with the use of our bodyweight, our legs or the reins in our hand. This may seem obvious but it requires considerable thought. Our use of sideways pressure must always complement our downward pressure aids: not everyone takes this on board when they ride or school their horse.

Giving in to gravity

Whether moving forwards, backwards or, to some extent, sideways, we should let gravity work for us. We must be careful not to block it. The majority of riders will have been doing this for ever without even thinking about it. It all happens so automatically, it is taken for granted.

Only, for some it doesn't work that way. Many riders resist gravity when they ride – tensions get in the way – and what they might do naturally on the ground fails to occur in the saddle. If this happens, horses can become confused and unsettled as normal patterns of behaviour are no longer made possible. This can lead to what tends to be described (often unjustly) as 'disobedience' and a lack of harmony all round.

Once riders slip behind the gravity line, they may resort to hauling on a tight rein and gripping up to stay on board.

By understanding and thinking more about our own weight aids – which over many generations have been studied and honed to help the horse become a willing partner – our riding can be greatly refined and improved.

Remember, the same principles, the same laws of Nature, govern us both – human and horse. However, if we are to take our riding to a

In shoulder-in, the horse remains bent as in the circle but, having angled our own upper body at approximately 35 degrees, the horse should mirror us as he moves laterally down the track.

higher level, it is time to study and understand the laws of gravity better. By learning more about these 'special effects' and how they assist in the aiding of the horse, we can now confidently expect to be totally at one and as one with the horse.

But first things first!

It should go without saying that when we ride, we must always carry ourselves in a good posture. Otherwise, how can the horse adopt a good posture?

You might be surprised at the sloppy position of some riders. Often this is done in the mistaken belief that sitting tall might lead to stiffness. That may be a risk, but it is far less harmful to horse or human than sitting crooked or slumped. In the latter, the more our weight shifts and slides, the more we remove the status quo, so the horse can no longer rely on us as a point of reference.

Copy the best

A quiet, firm seat is what we should aim for. We have an excellent example in Britain's leading competition riders and trainers: Charlotte Dujardin, Carl Hester and Richard Davison. From years gone by, the German Dr Reiner Klimke provided an outstanding example of the correct seat as does his daughter, Ingrid, today. The riders of the Vienna School and the Portuguese and Spanish Schools of Equestrian Art display the same style and elegance. There is nothing wrong in copying the best.

Basically, for straight, forward riding, we need to be as evenly balanced as possible. Keeping our eyes front, our seat and upper body should be aligned to the horse – in other words 'square to axis' – at all times. It is important to keep the stirrups evenly loaded coming down the centre line, but the moment there is a bend coming up, we will need to prepare the horse by making a slight adjustment into the inside leg. The experienced rider will do this naturally; the novice may have to be made more aware.

The more we sit up tall, the more we can let go of our weight.

Feel it!

Once we are confident in ourselves and our horse and are familiar with the conventional aids, developing a 'feel' for the weight aids should follow naturally. This will make us much less reliant on our hands.

Occasionally I like to stop in the middle of the school and release the reins for a moment or two. Don't do this with a horse you don't trust – but it is a nice way of taking the pressure off.

When you school your horse, tune into your body and mentally imagine the oft-mentioned plumb line, influenced by gravity, descending from the top of your head, down and through your centre to the ground. Somewhere, through the heart of your very core, joining you to the horse, you may feel it. Think about it, it is there! Become aware that you are not *making* this happen; it is part of you, happening to you – the power of gravity is at work. You just have to *allow* it to happen.

There is all the difference in the world between intentional changes of balance and of weight, and those that happen by accident. The first brings us to the subject of this book; the latter are often caused by a lack of core strength, the inability to direct the horse via the normal channels, or simply a crooked rider.

Busy hands, rounded back, calves that clamp, knees that turn out or favour one side, are all typical examples of a rider not in control of their bodyweight. For these riders it will be essential to improve their general seat and posture if they are later to master and perfect the techniques described in this book.

Another point I have noticed in recent years is that certain important tenets in riding — once automatically drummed into us — seem to have been forgotten or overlooked. It is as though 'the system' is failing to teach instructors the most basic of principles that have governed the riding of horses from as long as anyone can remember. One of those tenets concerns hips and shoulders. Cavalry training demanded that we ride with 'hips to horse's hips' as well as 'shoulders to horse's shoulders'. In my experience that is a very sensible premise and I might also add 'head to horse's head'. It is essential that both horse and rider are looking the same way.

While good riders generally put all this into practice — knowing or unknowingly — others may actually argue the opposite.

Finally, fashion dictates that a rider should at all times 'move with the horse'. It depends how we interpret this. Too many riders move irrespective of what the horse is doing. Instead, they set up a constant motion of their own, which may work against the horse's natural movement and even damage his back.

Instead, 'going with the movement' should mean that we ride with supple joints and allow ourselves to be carried forward without opposing or blocking the energy — unless intentionally. By sitting quietly, tall and upright with the shoulders back, elbows, knees and ankles bent, we learn to remain in balance so that the horse's movement is absorbed. This, in turn, allows the horse to come into balance with us, so that the two of us can become a partnership and there is no resistance.

Once this is accomplished, we are ready to go further and explore the individual weight aids. Some of these will be very familiar to you; others may prove a revelation. The main thing is to be aware of them since, whether or not you apply your weight knowingly, you can be absolutely sure the horse feels it in every direction, every gait and in every moment. Not only will these movements dictate what he *should* be doing but quite often what he *cannot do* — depending upon whether you, the rider, have made it possible or impossible. A horse is an animal of instinct; self-preservation makes it very hard indeed for him to oppose Nature's laws.

Shoulders to horse's shoulders; hips to horse's hips. Riding a circle requires us to align with the horse in every step. The rider will sit slightly deeper into the inside seatbone whilst the outside leg applies pressure behind the girth to keep the horse turning.

On a big-moving horse, canter can be energetic and daunting. It is better and safer to sit tall and above the energy source to control the balance.

Just before writing this, I was watching a Grand Prix rider school her horse. She rode over to me and asked me what I thought. I think she expected me to comment on her horse. Instead, I made a comment about her, as a rider. Fortunately, she wasn't at all offended and afterwards thanked me profusely. My few words of advice had – in a moment – completely transformed the way in which her horse was moving and the exercise she had asked him to perform. It happened to be the piaffe, but it could have been anything.

So what did I say? I said what was immediately apparent from the way in which her horse used himself

Not every rider knows to lighten their seat in piaffe. Sitting heavily will only hollow the horse and make it difficult for him to step underneath. The result is a poor piaffe which is light behind and heavy in front – not in accord with FEI principles, or, indeed, those of classical equitation.

behind. She was sitting too heavily and the horse was struggling. I explained how, in the piaffe, she would get a much better movement out of her horse if she lightened her weight from the back of the saddle and transferred more weight into her thighs. The driving seat requires more weight in the two seatbones, which may be all very well if you wish to gallop on – or extend the trot – but it can cause the horse to hollow. It is certainly not appropriate to the piaffe where the horse has to round his back, lower his haunches and bring his hind legs deeper underneath. This rider's horse had struggled to give her the movement she had requested but now, with his back freed up, he was able to give it gladly.

The same principle applies in almost every lesson I give. Not only do my eyes tell me when things could be improved; I 'feel' for them. I can only say that this empathy for how horses ought to be ridden comes from years and years of practical application. How could it be otherwise? That is why I would always advise serious riders to go to a trainer who has spent many years in the saddle, riding all sorts of horses, and who has the wisdom of experience at their fingertips.

It made me so happy to help that rider on that particular day as it was clear it was a lesson she would never forget. And it only took a few minutes to get across, first, because the rider clearly adored her horse, and second, because she was humble enough and open enough to know there is always something to improve. ■

Piaffe requires a very upright position, so that the rider's weight goes straight down through the middle of the horse and not into the back of the saddle, as is too often seen.

3 Natural Balance
Allowing Gravity to Work for Us

Riding big circles with the young horse requires a light seat and good inside leg support. The rider weights the inside stirrup at the girth for bend, while the inside thigh and knee applies a little sideways pressure to prevent the horse from falling in.

The moment a new student walks into the riding school, I generally have a good idea of how they are going to ride. They may be a novice or a professional, but posture and body language give away so much. How we move on the ground not only defines us as a person; it also affects our breathing, our well-being, our mood and our abilities.

Once we are in balance with ourselves, we have a much better chance of being in balance with the horse. The giving of the rider's aids depends very much upon a firm, steadfast but flexible seat. The horse will become muddled if everything is moving at once, therefore constancy of position is very important.

Only from a quiet seat can the young horse be taught to recognise the different aids and whether he is required to go forward, sideways, backward or remain on the spot. We must always be very clear in our own mind, how we ask and where we ask.

Still but effective

We must also recognise that the aids of seat, leg and hand will bring about a change of pressure on the horse's body. Whether or not this concerns his mouth, his back, or his sides, practically each and every aid we give will constitute a 'weight' aid.

For most of the time, our legs should hang quite naturally of their own weight – with or without stirrups. While the thighs form part of the seat to remain in contact with the horse, the lower legs should be in a neutral position at the girth. This allows us to give an aid – forward, back or against the horse's body – at a moment's notice.

Above *Riding the more mature horse out to the track requires a quiet inside leg at the girth, so the horse can gently flex to the inside to promote straightness behind.*

Only by sitting in the centre of the saddle with an approximately vertical pelvis will the rider be correctly aligned to let their legs drop. They will then have the freedom to move the legs forward or back as desired without losing balance.

It is too easy to resort to constant movement with the seat and legs. This nullifies their effect and can very quickly lead to a switched-off horse. Instead the seat and upper body should remain as quiet as possible, with the legs being used as sparingly as possible and always for a specific purpose. Only then can we train the horse to feel and recognise the different changes in pressure on his body, from both seat and legs and, in a much more subtle way, from the hands.

Be aware that every time we make a request, we are generally changing the status quo, even if only for a moment. This can either help or hinder.

When negotiating corners do not bring the inside leg too far back, or the horse may fall in on the shoulder. Instead, keep the inside hip forward and maintain bend with the leg at the girth or the horse may find it difficult to straighten.

The secret to the aiding process is to ask — and then release. In other words, weight down again, pressure reduced and so on.

Perfect position

Unfortunately, the perfect riding position, when demonstrated in a school situation, often looks stiff and unnatural. This can be caused by nerves, high expectations or simply an inability to let go.

There are other factors that can either help or hinder, for example:

● Rider's body shape.

● Horse's shape.

● Saddle shape.

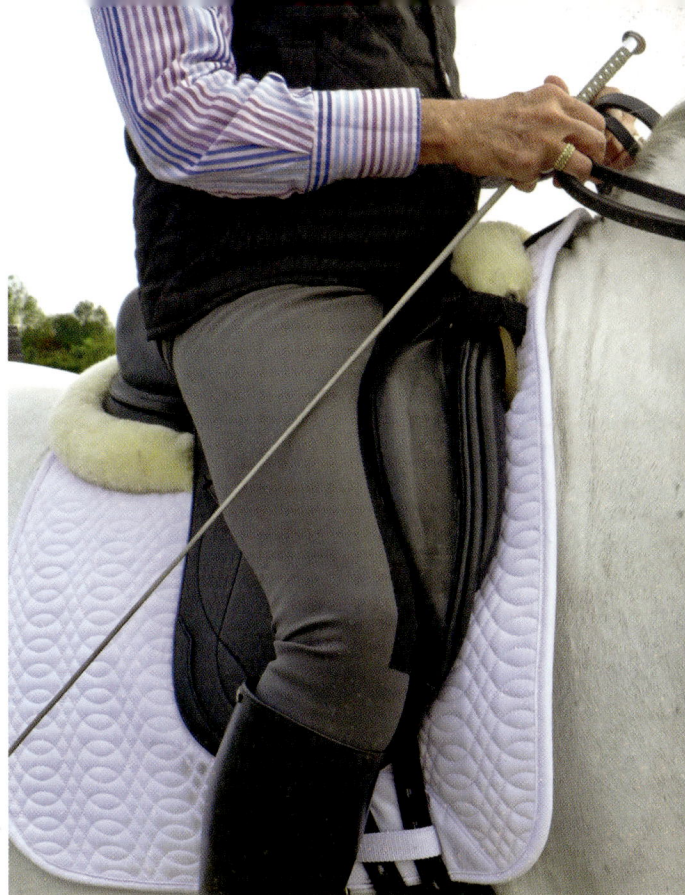

We will not ride well unless the saddle is comfortable and allows us to open our hips. Our legs can then drop more easily into the correct alignment, with the toe at the girth.

Most people believe that you have to learn a completely new balance when you ride a horse. Actually, I would beg to differ. The longer I live, the more I ride and train, the more I have come to realise that what happens to us when we mount up is governed by exactly the same physical rules and principles that cover us on the ground. In other words, what we do to stay upright, what we do to stay in balance, what we do to go forward is virtually the same, whether it's on our own two feet or over our horse's four feet. That is why the words of Xenophon, the Greek cavalry commander born in the fifth century BC, make so much sense: 'The man should sit astride the horse as though he is standing on the ground'.

Above *Sitting tall allows the horse the freedom through the back to maintain a light forehand, as required in the passage as shown.*

Below *Young people naturally sit up on horseback and this must never be discouraged.*

To sit or not to sit?

If riding students could take these wise words from the past on board, there could be radical improvement. The very words 'to sit' tend to give out the wrong message, unless very well explained.

Since we sit in an armchair, sit at our desks, sit in a lounger or in a backward-leaning car seat, too many riders fail to realise that the positioning of the pelvis in the saddle should be a very different matter.

- First, we should support ourselves – and sit up.

- Second, we should think of leading – rather than following.

Posture

Unfortunately, not everyone is very upright on the ground, so this may need to be addressed. Fitness is as important in riding as in any other sport, whether athletics, gymnastics, skating, martial arts and so on. Then, there could be issues with the horse. For example, a very small rider on a very big horse may find it almost impossible to straddle correctly, whilst an over-endowed rider may have balance problems.

Without core support it is very easy to slouch, which inhibits our ability to move easily and can so often turn the walk into a plod.

The most common problems tend to be:

● Lack of core strength.

● Stiffness in the hip joints.

● Lack of confidence, leading to tension and gripping.

These drawbacks, together with an uncomfortable saddle, may prevent a rider from settling into a deep, centred position, so time must be made available to deal with these issues. Whether help is sought in the gym, with a physio or by general self-improvement (or a combination of all three) matters little. The main challenge is to address the problem areas and think forward.

By this stage, what is now required from us on horseback may be far more natural and undemanding than most people will allow. There are far too many trainers and teachers out there who love to turn riding into a mystery. This is a pity since the rules are actually very simple.

They may not say so, but the best trainers generally help you to see in pictures what you need to do and feel. Time must be taken and self-belief plays an important part. See yourself trotting that circle, look down on yourself moving out to the track or making a transition, imagine you are the horse as you apply a leg aid – and anticipate his natural reaction to it ... and so on.

Tuning in to gravity

There is no reason why those who deport themselves easily on the ground should not automatically do the same on horseback. Generally speaking, the secret is to think 'up' – and take a pride in yourself. This will make you feel better in every way and hopefully put a smile on your face and that of your horse. The idea is to sit:

● Tall without being rigid.

● Central without being forced there.

● Deep without appearing to bear down or push.

All of which leads to confidence as a result of letting go of your tensions and weight.

A novice rider on a novice horse. This young rider naturally lifts her centre of gravity, which allows the horse to go freely forward.

What do I mean by 'letting go'? This is basically common sense, but often not discussed sufficiently in a riding school lesson. Fortunately, we have one huge asset in our favour – *the force of gravity*. The taller we sit, the more our weight drops away from us. We don't hold it up – instead we let it go. Quite naturally, gravity takes over.

Think of a guardsman on parade. To remain proud and stationary, he has no need to push actively against the ground to stay there. Instead he will be absolutely grounded simply by standing up. Indeed, the more he stands up the more he will be rooted to the spot. It's all very simple!

Why are more riding lessons not explained in this way? My first lesson was all about effort, squeezing, pushing with the seat, sticking like glue. Having to 'do' all the time (instead of sitting up and letting it happen) can be counterproductive. Generally, it is not comfortable for the rider or for the horse.

Above *Thinking tall on horseback is not dissimilar to standing tall on the ground – in both cases good posture leads to letting our weight drop straight down.*

Sitting tall does not necessarily indicate you are vertical. You have to be in the same balance as the horse, so whether he is making a very small circle (as shown here) or is more upright to move out, we should still mirror each other.

Depth of seat

It is therefore quite possible for a rider to sit in the correct posture, looking elegant and effective, whilst appearing to do very little indeed. Indeed the less we do, the more we acquire that depth of seat so admired in the top riders the world over.

The best and simplest expression that is used in countless disciplines, but most particularly in riding, has to be the one that everyone knows – *'What goes up must come down.'*

Once we get used to carrying ourselves with this in mind, we will be amazed how much easier it is to balance and feel secure in the saddle simply by letting it happen.

Work on the ground

Bearing all this in mind and built on my teaching experiences of the last several years, I have now come to the conclusion that the art of riding should first be taught on our own two feet.

It was for this reason that I began to run Weight Aid Workshops about twenty years ago and they have been a great success. For less

The shoulders back position naturally raises the rider's centre of balance which, in turn, helps the horse in the more collected movements.

Keeping the hula-hoop spinning can really help rider posture since it means raising one's centre of gravity. I also find it a very useful tool to free up the hips.

than half the cost of an hour's riding lesson, I hire a village hall for the evening and teach students the art of equitation on the ground ... and it works. We go through all the exercises from halt to rein-back, up to flying changes and the rest and the first thing students will explore during these movements is the art of natural balance and self-awareness.

How can anyone ride a horse if they are not aware of letting their weight down? Not only should this knowledge govern what we ourselves are doing; we will need to acquire it for the sake of the horse.

Few would argue that women tend to be more body-aware than men and they are also less likely to be embarrassed about exploring new sensations and discovering new approaches. I can safely attest to the fact that the most male students I ever taught on an Unmounted Workshop was three out of twenty-two. Brave souls!

Feeling our way

Not only should riders new to the discipline learn on their own two feet; it is also a wonderful refresher course even for experienced riders. I simply guide them through their weight aids. Generally, it's the simple exercises that need the most correction and cause the most excitement when everyone finds they work. Forward, halt, rein-back, circles, lateral exercises, counter-canter and so on. Great is the pleasure when students return home to find that thinking about their weight and reinforcing what they do naturally actually works for their horse too.

It is my earnest hope that there will come a time when all novice riders will be encouraged to have a lesson off the horse, prior to that first 'sit' on his back. In fact instructors should insist upon it – not just for the sake of the rider, but for the sake of the horse too.

After all, the theory of riding is as essential to our understanding as the practice itself, especially in the early days. It should all be logical, but some essential pointers that are often overlooked in a normal lesson would enhance the understanding enormously if first practised in this way.

Being connected to the horse is better understood once we can appreciate the fact it ties in with everything we do and feel on the ground. Yet this is rarely explained in a riding lesson, despite the fact it is totally logical.

Weighty matters

The term 'weight aids' helps us to pinpoint and explore the difference between allowing pressure (or weight) to drop as distinct from placing pressure against something, more or less in a horizontal plane.

We should never *force* our weight down when we ride a horse; it is something that should happen naturally – just as it does when we move around on our own two feet.

In the terminology I use in my Workshops, I refer to two types of weight/ pressure aid.

Above left *Quite unaware, riders will use both downward pressure and sideways pressure as they work their horse in the school. It's all part of the schooling process that develops into 'feel'.*

Above right *Moving into the smaller circle, the rider again deepens the inside leg, which still supports and invites the bend. It is very important not to collapse the inside ribcage.*

● First, there is 'downward pressure' – slightly exaggerated here.

● Second, we have 'sideways pressure'.

With the first, I demonstrate this by asking my students to listen to their footfalls on a wooden floor, first in walk, later skipping. Once I can get everyone to 'canter' or skip – right or left – they scarcely need to listen to the footfalls.

The taller they stretch, the more they can really feel the downward pull of gravity, and they seem surprised. Yet, in real life, we have been letting our weight down forever. And here we are not necessarily talking about upward and downward transitions, but all the various weight shifts required to bend, turn and move sideways. For example, in the act of turning right, we simply think 'step right' to turn right,

Working as a group, riders explore the different 'weight aids' on their own two feet. Riders learn to mimic on horseback what they would do naturally on the ground.

placing more weight into our right foot – and we do the opposite to turn left, and it happens. The effects of gravity and our sense of proprioception (the body's ability to sense stimuli relating to position, motion and equilibrium) simply take us that way. So why are riders not taught to think in similar terms on a horse?

Sitting up automatically lets our weight drop.

Cause and effect

Before we consider sideways pressure, I ask my students to work on the ground in pairs. We experiment how easy it is for them to bear down with their hands on their partner's shoulders without dislodging them – and how easy it is for that partner to remain in balance. I liken this to the horse bearing a balanced rider and how we can make things relatively easy for the horse simply by letting our weight down. The next stage is rather different. I ask one of the students to stand upright while their partner gives them a prod or push from the side. The sideways pressure applied in a surprise moment – even though it involves far less weight – nearly always unbalances them. Yet they were able to sustain much more downward pressure or downward weight without a problem.

When we grip up we interrupt the ability to work with gravity, which will affect the horse's balance too.

I then point out how much harder it must be for the horse, having sideways pressure constantly applied by busy legs. The words 'push him on' — must be a nightmare, whereas a still, calm seat with the weight of the rider dropping downwards and a mere quick tap at the girth will be perfectly acceptable.

Enlightenment

By allowing gravity to work through us we are much more secure than the rider who hangs on for dear life. It can be an enlightening moment when riders begin to realise that their seat will be even more secure once they can let go of their weight. Indeed, they begin to recognise it is a powerful aid. It requires little effort — quite the opposite. We simply let go!

These practical workshops also bring home to the rider how unsettling it can be to nag at the horse constantly with the legs. Yes, indeed, he can be nudged this way or that, but most people do too much. Instead, we need to use the sideways aids economically and they must always complement the downward weight aids.

Once we start to examine these nuances further, our natural reactions take on a whole new meaning. Each time the horse feels us drop our weight one way or the other, he will follow. It is his natural instinct to come with us. Out of self-preservation, he wants to come with us. He, too, is ruled by gravity and through him we are both connected to the ground. It is time surely to understand Nature's aids — our weight aids.

Riding without stirrups is the easiest way to 'let go' with the legs and to apply pressure only when required.

4 Our Basic Aids

Rein Effects and the Importance of Leg Position

Only when a rider has acquired the correct seat will they be able to handle the reins with discretion and apply the correct leg aids. We can only achieve straightness when the horse is able to bend more or less equally on both reins.

Although we are mostly looking for an even contact when we hack out, working in a school requires a much greater finesse to cope with the different movements and transitions required and to deal with the fact that there is always a corner coming up. Generally speaking, we must know how to flex or bend the horse to the inside on a bend, loop, turn or circle with a soft, inviting contact.

There must also be a very mild degree of bend when we ride 'out' to the track. This is to bring the horse's inside foreleg into line with the hind leg on the same side – the horse's shoulders being narrower than the quarters – to give the illusion of straightness.

Weight of the rein

Hand action must never be overt; just a soft asking feeling on one rein from the fingers should invite the horse to look this way or that. The flexion should come from the poll – never halfway down the neck, as is too often seen. The moment the horse responds the contact should normalise again.

Above *Riding out to the track always requires the horse to be slightly flexed to the inside with the rider's inside leg at the girth.*

Opposite *For the horse to bend on corners and circles, he will need to step well under himself with the inside hind. Here, my inside leg provides 'a pillar' for him to bend around at the girth.*

The inside rein placed against the base of the neck can also invite the horse to move out to the track or enlarge the circle, provided the outside rein gently opens.

In turning, circling or changing the rein across the school, most riders rely on the inside rein – also known as the direct rein. It is not necessary to open the hand away from the horse's neck, except with a very young or unschooled horse, unless there are mouth issues. Generally, both hands must remain as a pair but for each movement they will generally be required to act independently of each other.

At the same time, and in order to allow and support the action of the inside hand, the opposite or outside rein (generally known as the indirect rein) may check and confirm how much or how little the horse may bend to the inside. It can also be used to supplement a weight aid – placed against the base of the horse's neck to move the horse away from the pressure, as in a turn on the hocks, half-pass and canter pirouette.

In the collection of the horse, the weight of the rein alone was considered to be an aid in its own right in the days of the old classical Masters. This could only take place when the horse was so balanced, and so collected, that he scarcely required the presence of the hand to keep

The inside leg not only keeps the horse out to the track but, by weighting the outside (left) stirrup, he will also stay out even though he is looking to the inside.

him together. On a well-schooled horse, the very 'feel' of the rein, hanging of its own accord, provided sufficient contact.

Leg aids

The use of the legs must always support the action of the reins. Their placing on the horse's body is very important since every aid – however carefully applied – will exert a degree of weight or pressure. How the horse responds to these aids may be automatic or learned, but the fact remains that each 'ask', squeeze or push will make a difference to the horse's balance and manner of moving.

For most of the time, the knees and thighs should remain forward-facing, quietly cladding the horse as an extension of the seat. It is the job of the lower legs to issue requests, but for the most part they should drape the horse, the weight of the legs dropping naturally downwards.

Pressure should only be exerted when we need to ask for something

The smaller the circle, the more the horse depends on the weight aid of the rider's inside leg at the girth. The outside leg moves back to allow the outside of the horse's body to stretch accordingly.

Here the rider clearly lets the stirrup bear some of his weight. This allows the ankle and knee to flex – all of which keeps the rider firm but light in the saddle in the sitting trot. This is the classic 'leg at the girth' position.

different or for something to change – the most common request being the aid to go forward, make a transition or change direction.

Clearly, therefore, between each action of the lower legs, we should discipline ourselves to quieten them again. Gripping legs tend to deaden the horse's sides. The weight of our legs alone should keep our feet in the stirrups. As we have seen, it is gravity that keeps us sitting in the saddle and gravity also that assists us to drop the legs.

There are many different ways of applying the leg aids on horseback, but I am frequently shocked by the lack of understanding that concerns:

● Where the aid should be applied.

● How the aid should be applied.

● Which aid does what to the horse – and what the reaction should be.

Too often in a riding lesson, we hear the instructor shout 'Legs, legs, legs!' – and that is probably the most unhelpful instruction anyone can

Here, for the piaffe, the rider's legs move back behind the girth, to 'gather' the horse on the spot.

give, since every leg aid is different. There are, after all, several different pressure points and each can cause a different reaction. Throughout this book, we shall be discussing these and how our weight acts on each and every movement required of the horse. If an aid is incorrectly applied, it may make the horse do the absolute opposite of what the rider thought they asked for. This can only lead to conflict.

'Leg at the girth'

For the greater part of our work, the 'leg at the girth' position, should mean toe at the girth, or just behind. Feel your weight drop down into the stirrups, rather than pushing against them. You will keep your stirrups much more steady when you can 'let go' in this way, letting gravity work for you.

The heel should ideally be lower than the toe for normal work but for those whose feet have a high arch this can be difficult. Never forget that the weight-bearing part of the foot, which allows us to ease our position in the rising trot, and support the forward seat, both in hacking and jumping, is on the ball of the foot.

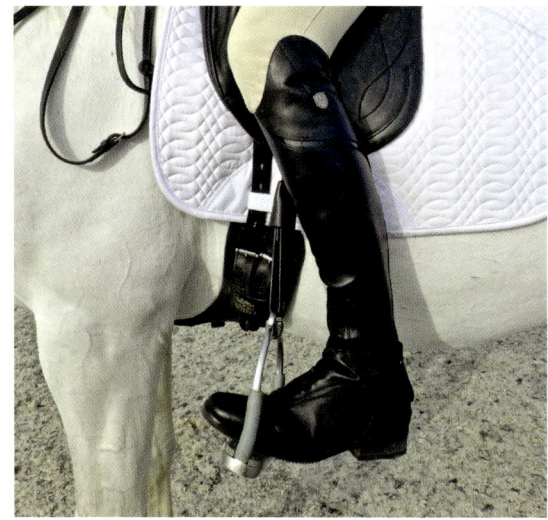

The 'leg at the girth' position generally refers to riding with the toe at the girth. The stirrup leather should remain roughly vertical as the rider's weight drops naturally downward. Any pushing against the stirrup iron counteracts the downward pull of gravity and may tense the back of the thigh and calf.

The request for the horse to go forward should be very simple. The girth area is very sensitive, owing to the influence of the intercostal nerves, which stimulate the horse to lift his back and engage his hind legs. In this position, he is best able to respond to most of our commands such as going forward, bending, making an upward transition and generally lightening the forehand.

It is much easier for novice riders to drop their legs into the correct position once they take up the rising trot. Pushing off from the stirrup – never the back of the saddle – allows them to develop a good rhythm as well as encouraging the lower legs to remain in place. The downward stretch through the front of the thighs will teach the rider to keep the knees low so there will be less inclination to grip up, which is not desirable.

Keeping the fork lightly in contact with the saddle is also important for balance. 'Riding on the fork' is often used as a term of derision – the implication being that all the rider's weight rests there – but this should never be the case. We don't sit on the fork (we sit on the seatbones)

Here the horse shows excellent engagement in response to a correct leg aid. For perfection the neck should be a little longer.

This novice rider will rise more effectively by folding a little more at the hips, but by weighting the stirrups and looking through her horse's ears, she is making good progress and going with her horse.

but this third point of contact allows us to stretch the legs down through the front of the thighs, which assists our stability. It is then much easier to sit straight and deep with the knees low and in good contact with the horse – neither gripping nor tensing up.

Legs back

Unfortunately and all too frequently, riders' legs can be observed placed too far back at all times. This will leave the horse unsupported through the shoulders and may cause him to lean, hollow his back or lose engagement behind. It also reduces the rider's security and ability to use their seat to best effect. Furthermore, there will be constant tension that stymies forward movement. In other words, once the rider starts to grip up, impulsion and balance are lost. Since the aid to halt requires the rider's legs to *close behind the girth* why, when the horse is expected to go forward, does no one bother to correct this glaring rider mistake?

With the legs continually applied behind the girth in this way it is almost impossible not to put unwarranted pressure both on the rider's fork and on the horse's sides. This imbalance would account for the unpleasant sight of horses swinging their quarters about or backing up when waiting their

Here the rider transfers more weight to the front of the saddle for a downward transition.

Nagging legs – unfortunately a common sight in all disciplines.

turn at a show or a jumping competition. If only the riders would sit up and remain central, their legs could drop! Then their horse might stand still.

Leg questions

How many riders understand that every time they move one leg (or both) forward or back, it changes the pressures of their seat in the saddle?

Above left *The rider demonstrates how a lack of support from the inside leg applied too far back allows the horse to drop onto the forehand.*

Above right *Here the rider sits up, applies the leg at the girth and the horse is immediately lightened and balanced.*

Without meaning to, many riders are giving the horse a different weight aid each time – but are they aware they have done so? These may or may not be appropriate.

How many riders mentally separate the aids of the lower legs from those of the thighs? If the thighs are not stable, the seat will be less so.

How many riders appreciate that their knees need to remain deep and in place if they are to act as effective 'hinges' to the use of the lower legs?

Leg effects on the seat

It is generally accepted that there can be no balanced seat if the rider's legs act in the wrong place. While the thighs form part of the seat, it is the rider's lower legs that generally apply the aids. Yet such is the horse's sensitivity, every movement we make will have an effect above and below the saddle. Small changes in the balance of our pelvis can make a huge difference to how the horse feels us on his back.

For example, with the rider sitting upright in the centre of the saddle:

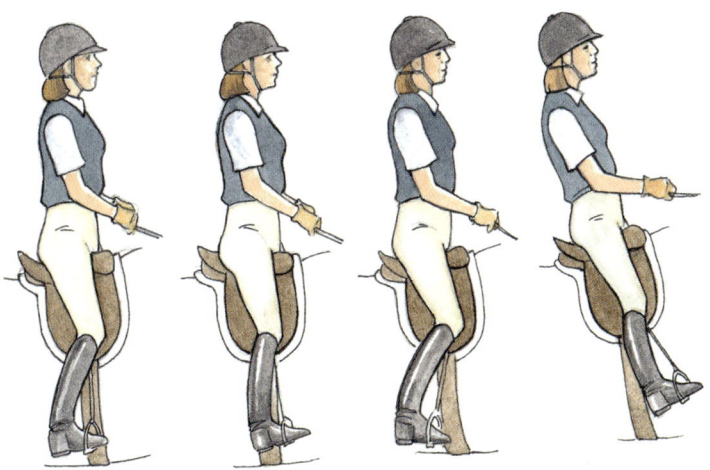

Above *A nice forward balanced trot, much helped by the rider's leg remaining quietly at the girth.*

- Both legs relaxed and with the lower legs hanging roughly vertical – toes aligned with girth – the rider should be in a 'neutral' position – *weight in saddle remains central.*

- Both legs moved forward an inch or so in front of the girth – rider will sit more on the seatbones – *weight spreading towards back of saddle.*

- Both legs a hand or more behind the girth – *less weight on seatbones, more on front of saddle.*

- Both legs a hand or more in front of girth – *weight slipping backward – 'armchair position'.*

Unless the rider is balancing on the stirrups and taking the forward seat (as in jumping, etc.) the shorter the stirrup leathers, the more the rider's seat will be forced backwards, which will place too much weight on the horse's weakest point.

Pressure off

The trick in the giving of any command – especially to go forward or stop – is to ask with the appropriate seat aids, and then allow. This is only possible with a balanced seat. If we are not passive in between times, these signals will become meaningless. If the legs are constantly 'on', the poor horse will be denied the time to listen. No wonder so many become 'dead to the leg'.

The classical aids are those that work on the anatomy and physiology of the horse. As with the human body there are certain trigger points, tickly points or reactive points, and we need to learn where these are located.

The term 'weight aids' may sound complex but the theory is not complicated. It is simply a question of recognising pressure added or reduced by different applications of weight and using this to our advantage. Horses are sensitive creatures but too often we use pressure against them – as already explained above. This can lead to real abuse – where the horse *tries* to give us what we want, but too often, the way in which we asked was flawed and actually works against Nature.

Sensitive riders will generally know when they have 'blocked' their horse; the insensitive do not. The horse is punished for not being able to carry out a certain movement, a certain task and more and more pressure is applied. Once a rider understands and appreciates just how to let their weight down, they are halfway there.

Forward with ease

Only when we are seated in the middle of the saddle will we feel centred and in tune with the horse. This allows us the good balance required to ride with minimal aids so the horse's mouth, back and sides are spared and we can both enjoy the work.

These changes in our demeanour may be small and unobtrusive, but they are so logical. If we think back to how we move on the ground, the answers are all there. We want to turn right – so we step right; on the horse we merely put more weight into the right seatbone and/or the right stirrup. It is a given that the horse comes with us. The thinking is the same, the feeling is the same and the result is the same.

We want to go straight ahead. We have equal pressure in both seatbones and both stirrups, the horse moves straight.

We want to move back. We gently tip the pelvis just as we would to walk backwards ourselves and the horse moves away from pressure to move back with us.

The use of pressure can transform the way of going for the horse –

Opposite *Releasing the horse from the pressure of the lower leg makes it much more inviting for him to move freely forward.*

but the 'off' moment is as important as the 'on'. We just need to remind ourselves of it.

Basically, we need a holistic appreciation of the horse's balance. By developing our sense of awareness, we understand and act upon what needs support, what needs to be freed up and how in every moment of every movement, our balance and our weight is for the horse. ■

Opposite *The more we can 'let go' with our legs and ride the horse forward more by thought than action, the easier it will all become. When riding becomes subliminal it is hard to spot any aids at all.*

5 The Weight Aids of the Rider's Seat

Our Invisible Aids

The seatbones and their effects are not always explained to riders in the average riding lesson. To ride better, some understanding of anatomy is helpful. How many riders realise that we cannot be stable in the saddle unless the entire underside of the seat is in contact with the saddle to a greater or lesser degree? Rocking onto the seatbones and losing contact in front will destabilise the whole structure above and below the waist. Perching on the fork and losing contact through the buttocks blocks the rider's back and will place the horse on the forehand.

A nice central upright seat makes it so much easier for the horse to carry us correctly.

The perfect seat?

Riding schools are notorious for teaching what they perceive to be the 'perfect position' but this can be deeply flawed. It may look very nice when we can draw a neat line downwards from the top of the rider's hat, through the ear, to the shoulder, to the hip, to the heel and thence to the ground but what if the rider is not in the centre of the saddle?

When we sit in the vertical in the lowest part of the saddle we should clearly feel a sense of gravity passing straight down through us to the ground. This unites us with the horse.

The more misguided instructors insist on the rider bringing the lower legs too far back, which only throws the student off balance. This tends to place the rider on their fork – with the horse leaning on the forehand – or worse, the 'armchair' seat, where the rider's weight drifts towards the weakest part of the horse's back, causing him to hollow away from the pressure. In either case the horse is unable to track up and lift his back correctly and the rider is no longer able to 'lead the dance'.

The forward seat

When hacking, jumping or schooling the young, old or sensitive horse, the forward seat is the natural way to go. It frees up the horse, allowing him to use his energy to go forward. Balanced on thighs, knees and stirrups the rider can give the horse's back a 'break'. Most horses enjoy a few good 'blasts' around the school with the rider off their back, first thing. Then they can settle more easily to the more exacting work .

The forward seat is not considered appropriate for dressage since the exercises expected require the horse to be balanced on his hocks, not on the forehand. Obviously, as we start off the young horse's education, we will sit lighter. Then, as we introduce more and more exercises over time there will be a gradual change to a full-seated position.

Right top *Even in dressage, we should regularly give the horse's back a break. Rising trot is an important part of the warm-up, but taking more weight into the stirrups in canter is very beneficial too. Think of dropping your weight into your knees and thighs rather than into the saddle, and feel the difference.*

Right bottom *Sitting full seated should never mean pushing or bearing down. The more we sit up, the easier it is for the horse to step under and the more we centralise our weight.*

Horses get tired if always ridden in one fixed way or outline, so there will always be times when the horse is allowed to stretch actively on the long rein from well-engaged hind legs. In this way, we freshen up and ease those muscles that have supported us so well and time spent on the long rein is rarely wasted. Indeed, it is important to the muscle-building process and should intersperse our schooling time on a regular basis.

Sitting up into halt is an effective way of allowing the horse's back to come up to meet the rider as the horse steps under with his hind legs.

For most of the work with a mature horse, a central and upright position in the saddle is generally the best balance for both rider and horse in all the school movements including the halt. Our main concern is never to block the horse with unwanted pressure and to remember that the weakest part of his back is just behind the cantle.

Sitting tall

It is common sense that the more upright we are in the saddle, the more balanced we ourselves become. We talk about sitting, but it would make more sense to think of 'standing' – as prescribed by Xenophon – and then easing down into the saddle through flexible hips, knees and ankle joints. It is important always to remain in the centre of the saddle, which requires good core support and the ability to open the shoulders. Work on the lunge will help this.

Sitting tall allows our weight to drop naturally through the centre of the saddle, down through the front of the thighs, into the knees and thence to the stirrups.

The result of a good seat is the preservation of the horse's back and this is a beautiful thing. The more balanced we become, the more balanced our mount; nevertheless, we both need all the help we can get. A comfortable saddle for you as well as the horse is important – so beware of those with a high, narrow twist which may hurt or push you backwards.

Three legs give stability unlike a two-legged structure – as in a rocking chair.

The three-point seat

Once sitting in the middle of the saddle, our weight can then flow naturally down over the front of our thighs into the knees and thence to the stirrups. It is worth working at this as pushing against the stirrups is detrimental to the seat. The balance we feel through the three-point seat is not so different from that of a three-legged stool. By starting from a position of centred stability we can then develop a language of invisible seat aids.

Once the rider's knees are facing straight ahead, and the legs 'hang' free from tension, the feeling of connection to the horse through the seat is liberating. By sitting upright and tall in the centre of the saddle, the rider should become aware of a triangular base of support that gives stability and balance to the whole. The rider should feel the following:

- The two seatbones – to the rear – often referred to as the 'knobbly bits'.

- The ischial ridge that forms the right and left branches of the triangle – less easy to feel.

- The central pubic bone (or fork) at the front of the triangle where the two edges of the seat meet up together – easy to feel if leaning forward – 'just there' if sitting straight.

This illustration shows a contact throughout the underside of the pelvis. The weight is more prominently at the rear of the pelvis and, in front, the fork has just a very mild contact.

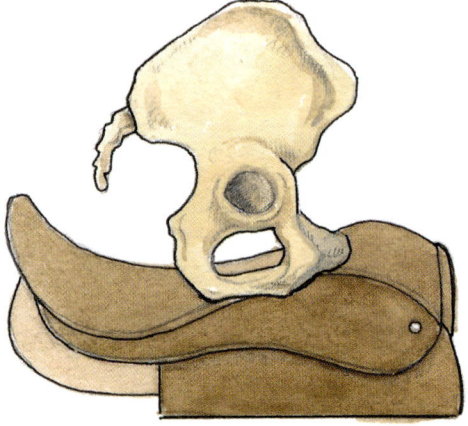

This has come to be known as the three-point seat. When riding astride It gives a feeling of perfect balance and support to the whole body from front to back. With the entire underside of the seat now in contact with the saddle, stability is achieved so that the seat may become 'quiet' yet still able to issue minute but important shifts of pressure. The weight aids of the seat should be quite invisible.

When we sit in a dressage saddle, our position should naturally be vertical. Here there is clearly a full contact from front to back of the rider's pelvis, which allows the rider to remain deep and centred.

For me, this is the kindest seat for the horse, since the rider's weight is now over the horse's strongest point as well as close to his centre of balance.

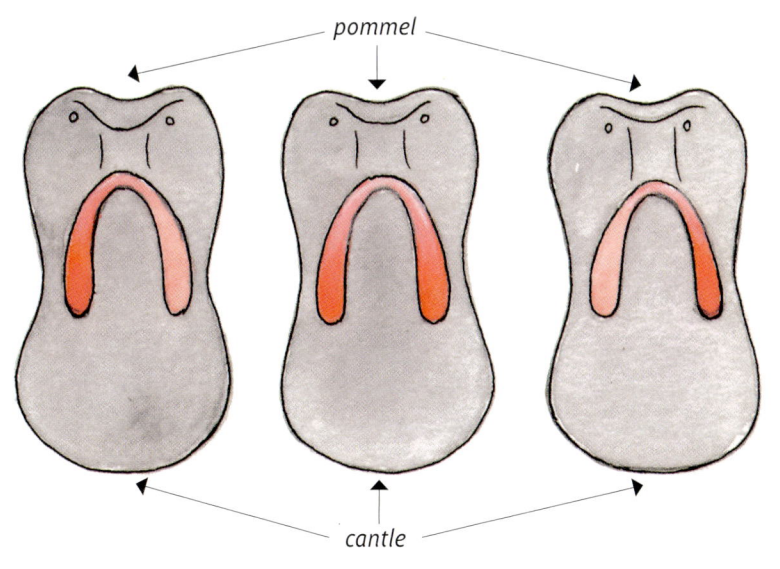

pommel

cantle

Turning left   Forward and straight –   Turning right
weight central

The three-point seat is the best way of describing the base on which we sit in the saddle. There will be more weight on the two seatbones to the rear and just a mild contact with the crotch at the front. Without that triangular base there can be no real stability.

Bad backs

It is of concern when riders are instructed to 'tuck their tail under'. This rounds the back, denies the spine its natural spring and elasticity and reduces the support system. Should the rider then wish to halt or prevent themselves from slipping backwards in movement, they will need to rely more and more upon the reins.

'Going with the movement' should be virtually invisible. Unfortunately for the horse, it is often promoted as a busy, thrusting seat, which might be useful in an emergency, but if used generally will lead to back pain both in horse and rider. When the pelvis is tilted behind the vertical (below left), the spine rounds and contact is lost from the front of the saddle. The majority of the rider's weight now shifts towards the cantle, height is lost, together with stability. We are not built to walk or run in such a posture – why do it on a horse?

'Tail under' – *A collapsed upper body causes the back to round and the pelvis to slip behind the vertical thus over-burdening the horse's weakest point with little or no support from the rider's legs.*

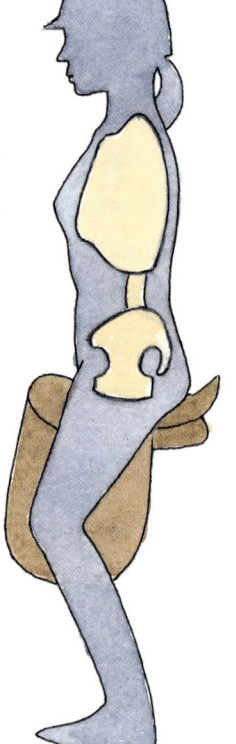

'Upright seat' - *The ideal dressage seat requires the upper body to be erect with a vertical pelvis in full contact with the centre of the saddle. The majority of the rider's weight is directed towards the horse's strongest point supported by a good leg position.*

Directing our weight

With good core support, the pelvis should remain more or less upright for all our sitting work, making contact with the saddle from front to back. Tilting it forward will lighten your seat and, while this is important for hacking and the schooling of young or fragile horses, generally the vertical seat is best. It is favoured by top dressage riders all over the world.

Once we are centred, we should be in a firm, balanced position in the centre of the saddle. While our seatbones bear most of our weight, we must also allow it to drop down over the front of our thighs into the knees and into the stirrups. This should keep us grounded and safe.

Sitting 'above' the movement with more weight in the stirrups on a very fresh horse is wise advice. In the event of a spook or shy, we are less likely to lose balance and thus the sooner the horse will want to join up again. He must come to us, not us to the horse.

To stay in balance, think also of spreading the weight from front to back and you will discover just how sensitive the horse will be to any changes of pressure. For the most part, our seatbones should remain in the centre of the saddle — not at the cantle as is too often seen. Certain types of horse will require a carefully fitted saddle that is built up to place the rider centrally over the strongest part of his back.

The rider sitting up tall with good core support can only help the horse to raise his back and step underneath himself.

Upright and balanced! Despite riding in the UK for over fifteen years, I did not really capture the feel of the classical seat until I sat in a Portuguese saddle like this one.

Seat aids

The words ' push with the seat' can be very harmful to both the rider's back and that of the horse if they are not properly understood. Instead, sit still but again, experiment with letting more weight down through the front of the saddle for collecting, slowing down, going to halt or reining back. Then try the opposite – putting more weight on the seatbones – to send the horse forward. Keep everything very subtle and you will discover nuances you may never have thought possible before. Your legs energise the horse; your seat shows him how and where that energy should go.

Left top *By lifting the ribcage, bringing the shoulders back and sending the seatbones forward, we are in the best position to ask for medium or extended trot. This takes pressure off the fork and 'opens the door' for the horse to flow through!*

Left bottom *By sitting more vertical with our weight closer to our horse's centre of gravity the horse will naturally collect and move more upwards in the gait – as we slightly 'close the door'.*

'Bridging the gap'

On a very sensitive or forward-going horse I tend to think of my seat forming a bridge. By sitting up and not pressing down, I allow the energy to flow forward and through as it is offered from behind. To increase the flow of energy, opening the shoulders and bringing them slightly behind the vertical will deepen the seatbones and send the horse forward and onwards. We often see this in dressage competitions in the extended gaits.

When it comes to gathering up or collecting the gait, we still need activity – often more – but we reverse the process by sitting deeper into the thighs to reduce the pressure in the seatbones. Taken to the extreme, this shift of weight away from the back of the saddle can be used to shorten the gait, to half-halt, to collect, to passage, or even to contain the horse on the spot – as in piaffe.

Teaching the horse to collect involves a subtle gathering together of all these feelings combined. Too often we see riders using their hands to achieve collection, but it is far more subtle than this. First we need energy. By taking charge of that energy with our weight aids, we are masters of the horse's balance before the energy has reached the forehand.

We will know when we have got this right when the horse remains energetic behind, but light in front – attentive to our each and every request.

Turning and moving sideways

Weighting the seatbones independently of each other is a very important aid. In turns, circles, lateral work and so on, these weight aids must be discreet and unobtrusive and the rider must remain vertical. So, to turn right, a little more pressure on the right seatbone will draw the horse right; to turn left, transfer the pressure to the left seatbone. Leaning is all very well in showjumping when working at speed; in dressage it should rarely be seen except in an unexpected moment. Basically, we want the horse to bend around our inside leg to turn in or keep him out to the track. We also need to work with the horse as upright as possible since leaning will only negate the balancing process. It is also very important that, having finished a movement or turn, we then return to 'neutral' again so our weight drops down 50:50 into both seatbones.

It is the role of the outside rein and outside leg to move the horse away from pressure in the turn on the hocks, on ever-decreasing circles and in the canter pirouette. Here, the rider sits very tall to keep the horse in balance.

Support system

To preserve our own back, our core muscles play an important role. We must never forget to open and square our shoulders to produce enough flexion through the back to go 'with the movement'. We should also carry

our head and neck proudly, erect but never stiff. Think of the crown of the head being the highest point, then drop your chin. This should complement what we ask of our horses, who should be poll high, dropping their nose and relaxing the jaw.

The great Masters always talked about a proud upper body. Mestre Nuno Oliveira of Portugal promoted the idea of 'inflating the torso' by opening the ribcage. The late Sally Swift spoke of 'centering'. To stay in balance we need core strength as well as firm, toned thigh muscles. This requires a certain degree of fitness.

Collection or gathering the horse is all to do with raising our own centre of gravity and drawing the horse up and forward. We sit deep but we sit up.

Imbalances

Unless a rider has developed good core strength, the pelvis will generally tend to tilt back to find the lowest point in movement. Acceleration may cause the knees to rise and the upper body to collapse. The more the horse steps forward, the more the rider's weight and balance drifts towards the cantle. This subsequently impairs the horse's loins and prevents him stepping through from behind.

The inevitable result of the 'armchair seat' is that riders who have sat like this all their lives will inevitably end up with a bad back themselves. We are not built to walk or ride with a tucked-in pelvis – it rounds the back and denies us of spring.

Good core support not only helps our position in the saddle, but also helps to protect our back when we ride.

Unbalanced riders tend to support themselves with the reins in a vain attempt to stay central. Our centre of balance is roughly just under the breastbone – which makes it important to sit tall and square. The horse's centre of gravity lies at a point roughly just below the saddle flap where the girth is done up and if the rider can stay aligned above this point, the destabilising effects of acceleration and centrifugal force are much reduced.

This is a typical armchair seat where the rider props themselves up on the cantle and rounds their back. This can lead to severe discomfort and hollowing in the horse's back.

Students new to the discipline – or even those who are experienced – should be encouraged to ride without stirrups to gain a deeper seat. This involves sitting up with relaxed hip joints so the seat can 'open' around the horse.

Once the stirrups are taken up again, there will be less pressure on the front of the saddle and more weight in the rider's seatbones, which should remain in the centre of the saddle. This is correct. The fork merely acts as a steadier, generally applied in downward transitions and the rein-back. (Also in some of the airs above the ground, but this is for later.)

Young and older horses

Every horse is different, but for most young horses and the old-timers, it helps to lighten the back of the seat in an upward transition by gently tipping the pelvis forward to take more weight in the knees and stirrups.

With a more mature horse, think of extending the gaits by tipping the pelvis very slightly in the opposite direction so that the seatbones can engage and send the horse forward.

Some people think 'down' to halt. Instead, think of sitting very upright and very central, which will 'catch' the impulsion before it has travelled through to the forehand. If you think 'up' to halt and lift the ribcage at the same time, this unites the horse to you.

Always think 'up' into halt.

Final thought

It is very easy for riders keen to progress up the scales of training to forget the horse! Yes, we want our horse to do this or that, but do we take time to understand how our bodies impact on his? We need to understand the different 'feels' in order to adjust our weight and make it easier for him. Tuning in will make us much more aware of the influences of the seat. The triangular base upon which we sit not only gives us stability, it gives us other 'gears' and other choices.

As already discussed, we will sit more on the two seatbones and less on the fork for our normal forward movements. Then, as our demands grow and we introduce collection, the rein-back, canter to halt, changes and the higher airs – we will discover new feelings and new balances that we might never have considered before. All dictated to us by the horse! ■

All horses enjoy the chance to let off steam, when the rider takes their weight forward and off their back.

6 Straightness, Forward and Back

Pressure On – Pressure Off

R emember – we may well know where we are in space, but do we know 'where' and 'how' our horse is and how he feels us on his back?

At the onset of riding, many horses will naturally move off on the forehand. They may be straight but it will take time to develop good balance.

People are quick to say 'my horse is on the forehand' – but do they stop to think it may well be that they themselves are on the forehand and the horse has no opportunity to pick himself up until we do the same?

It is ironic to think that the more he is in tune with us, the more our horse will show up our faults. To ride well, we need to realise that he will generally mirror us in each and every movement, and while we may have many strengths, it is likely we also have weaknesses. Even the best rider in the world won't be perfect; few are evenly balanced when they ride.

A good, forward, working or collected trot again relies on the correct inside leg position able to act at the girth.

It is a sobering thought therefore that every little thing we do will either help or hinder, whatever our intentions. This puts the ball firmly back in our court. Generally, we are responsible for how our horse moves, how he carries us and how he progresses.

Below *Rising trot not only spares the horse's back provided we land lightly – it can also help improve the balance and desire to go forward for both young or older horses – or those who are simply not very forward-thinking.*

When pressure means 'go!'

The first and most important aid we give the horse in riding is to teach him to go forward. A quick squeeze from both legs acting at the girth stimulates the intercostal nerves, which act to elevate the horse's shoulders and free up the back. The horse is very sensitive to this form of pressure – he is often ticklish around the girth area – so the swift application of the legs here should make him want to go forward. Some might deduce that he is escaping from the pressure and his reward will be a cessation of the aid – in other words, pressure off. Others would see this as a learned response to the pressure aid. Whatever the case, a wise rider does not continue to ask and ask again. Instead, the horse should be rewarded through a giving of the hands as well as a giving, or cessation, of the rider's leg aids when he moves off. Clear-cut aids – ask and then release – should very quickly result in a willing horse.

If, with the more phlegmatic horse, the initial request is not obeyed, then it will be necessary to ask again with a little more pressure – but make it quick. Sudden pressure is much more effective than slow, stifling pressure. If that makes no difference, a quick tap with the stick behind your leg rarely fails.

A 'taking' hand will lead to an unwilling horse, as will a 'taking' seat. Unfortunately, there are many different ways to discourage a forward-going horse and these are all too common. Riders who continually push with their seat can grind on the horse's back and generally make things very uncomfortable. Any to-and-fro action is not good for the horse – it often 'strings him out' – and is equally bad for the rider's back. It is most unlikely to produce more forwardness.

Thinking forward

For the horse to make a simple upward or downward transition he must have the freedom to push from behind. Both processes should involve engaging his hind legs further underneath his body to take the weight back. In both cases, the horse's neck should be arched, with the head approximately in the vertical. It is a mistake to pull the head in or 'shorten' the neck – so prevalent in dressage today – since this blocks the shoulders and places the horse on the forehand.

A schooled horse should require very little pressure from the rider's legs once he has been fully worked in. Here, the rider will gradually give more with the rein to lengthen the neck as the horse settles.

This young mare offers a calm forward walk much assisted by the rider gently easing her seat forward, combined with an asking leg at the girth.

Having halted or slowed, bringing our own shoulders just behind the vertical allows us to engage our seatbones ready to send the horse forward. As the legs ask, the upper body must allow. It is important that riders can be flexible through the lower back to allow this process to take place.

In the case of a younger horse, we should compensate for his weakness by lightening the seat. Even if we remain sitting, we can take more weight into the thighs, knees and stirrups to allow him more leverage.

In the early days, leaning a little forward and moving forward to rising trot helps reinforce the desire for action. Sitting trot is not ideal for young horses with tender backs, although more and more people do it nowadays. However big or strong the horse may appear in his early years, maturity can still be far off. Sitting into the horse or pushing can reduce his natural eagerness to work and may lead to back problems – including kissing spines – at a later stage.

Legs on

There are still too many riders who 'hang on' to the horse with their legs all the time. Instead, they should keep the thighs and knees snugly in contact and parallel to the horse, while allowing their lower legs to drop naturally of their own weight. Turning the knees out disturbs the cladding effect of the rider's legs and there will be the temptation to grip up. Too much pressure with the legs dulls and stultifies the horse and it is very important to reward every attempt at forwardness with a release of pressure.

The aid to go forward should be very quick, and released the moment the horse responds.

Always think:

● Legs on for a moment to go forward.

● Legs off the moment he does.

In this way the horse enjoys the sense of going forward freely rather than being hampered by legs that hold on and impede. Think of your weight falling away from you, into the stirrups and thence down to the ground. That way you will keep your stirrups without the need to push against them.

When, for example, you want greater forwardness in trot or canter, try not to impede your horse with stronger and stronger leg aids. Often it is the succinct touch at the girth that encourages him to throw his elbows out and offer more. Once he is going forward nicely, it often helps to bring your shoulders back so that your seatbones engage more deeply and drive the horse forward. This is particularly effective for medium trot or canter, provided the horse is on his hocks to start with.

A lovely straight trot, with the rider sitting up quietly and letting her legs drop.

When pressure means 'stop!'

It is a serious fault for a rider to ask for forwardness with their legs placed too far back. Legs set well behind the vertical tilt the rider's pelvis forward and this puts pressure on the rider's fork. This, as discussed in the previous chapter, is a slowing down or stopping weight aid. In addition, squeezing with the legs behind the girth raises the horse's back behind the saddle instead of lifting the forehand. This makes it difficult for the horse to go forward in balance.

A promising attempt at a square halt, with the riders sitting up and dropping both legs just behind the girth. Gradually the horse will learn to close up behind.

Too many lessons concentrate on 'legs back, horse forward'. Often this means a battle of wills, with the horse unsupported through the forehand.

Bearing down with the seat – a negative weight aid – is as disconcerting for the horse as a seat that moves about too much. The horse will tend to shrink from this type of pressure and hollow his back. The hind legs are then less able to step underneath, so any inclination on the part of the horse to move forward or to halt in balance is nullified. Forcing him forward by a continual use of spurs or stick is something else I disdain.

When pressure means 'back!'

Just as the legs can ask the horse to move forward, they are also instrumental in moving the horse backwards. Legs back involves weight back, so it is natural for the horse to try to pick us up – even if he has never been taught to do so. He simply wants to be united with us again.

Once the lower legs move from their 'hanging ' position to being placed a few inches behind the girth, it changes the feeling of the rider's seat on the horse's back. Suffice to say, moving both legs back in this manner and squeezing is an invitation for the horse to follow. In such a case, he backs up in order to rebalance and step under us.

Sometimes, we may have deliberately asked him to do this; at other times, we may be unaware that we have asked. It is very sad when we see a horse being told off by a rider who has applied this aid without realising what they are doing. It happens a lot at the start of a race or a competition.

Rein-back – 'opening the door behind'

In the same way that we close the legs for halt, a correct rein-back is achieved by closing both legs about a hand's breadth behind the girth to draw the quarters under. By sitting gently on the fork, we effectively close the door to forwardness and open the door behind.

Having taken our shoulders slightly forward we are now sitting more on the front of the saddle, which lightens the weight in our seatbones and makes it easier for the horse to move back and step through without impediment.

Simultaneously, the hands should close around the reins, which must be short enough for the horse to feel the aid and relax his jaw without any sense of pulling. The hands must never move back. Instead, there should be a soft 'asking' feeling through the reins, complemented by a similar feeling of 'asking' through the rider's lower legs behind the girth. In this way the horse can then be guided, very naturally and gently, to step back.

There is nothing worse than rushing the horse in the rein-back. We avoid this by sitting a little deeper in front – our weight dropping down through the front of the thighs, into the knees and thence to the ground – to keep everything steady. The movement is then requested step by careful step without shortening the neck.

From top to bottom

Preparing the horse for rein-back requires the horse to stand as square as possible.

Moving the rider's lower legs back puts more pressure on the front of the saddle, which 'closes the door' in front and 'opens the door' behind.

Once pressure is applied to the horse's sides behind the girth, he will naturally move into the space by stepping backwards.

At the onset of training, the horse should be rewarded if he manages even half a step. If all goes well, this will develop into several steps over time.

Rein-back can be very difficult for some horses. A sympathetic rider will lighten their weight off the back of the saddle and concentrate it into the stirrups (as shown). On the right rein there is real resistance; on the left the rider achieves one step on a gentle contact. It may take several months to train properly on both reins and should always be developed one step at a time.

The most important thing is to make the exercise comfortable for the horse. It is very easy for the horse to feel bewildered or blocked in the rein-back. Many horses will have suffered bad experiences as this is a movement that is not always performed correctly, even at higher level dressage. Too many riders simply rely on the reins without applying the correct seat and leg aids. I have been horrified by some of the rein-backs seen in competition riding, where the rider sits hard into the back of the saddle and pulls back with the reins. This makes it almost impossible for the horse to step backwards correctly and it is no surprise when horses ridden this way hollow and resist.

With more pressure transferred to the front of the seat, there is no excuse for discomfort or tension. All my horses enjoy the rein-back especially as we follow it up with a transition to something they enjoy such as passage or canter, where I would obviously change the seat aids. It is so much easier for the horse to move off in balance when the rein-back has placed him more onto his hocks.

As the horse begins to recognise the work discussed in this chapter, he should gradually require less and less leg pressure as our aids become more refined. Never forget that it is the combined effect of our weight in the seat, the thighs and the lower legs that develops that special language of the weight aids. ■

Rein-back sets the horse up for passage and the higher-level work. The most important thing is always to go forward after working in rein-back.

7 How the Horse Moves into Pressure

Bend, Crookedness and Rider Impact

The horse cannot readily resist the weight aid of a correctly placed inside leg.

$\mathbf{I}$t was such a big discovery when I began to understand the role of the inside leg in riding; I can only marvel that it had never meant very much before. Looking back, maybe I just didn't think about it very much. As a child, I just got on and rode, but while I did worry about getting the correct canter lead on the centre line of a dressage test, none of the teachers at Pony Club had offered any solutions. It is only when I entered the world of teaching and training that I realised there is a lot more to the weight aids than meets the eye.

Circles

The beauty of circle work is not only the effect it has on the horse, but also how it improves the rider. It teaches awareness and body control. In the riding school or dressage arena, the ideal scenario is when we use both types of pressure – downward or lateral – sparingly. For example, on a circle we should be aware of placing a little more downward pressure into the inside stirrup placed at the girth to draw the horse into the correct bend. However, almost a second later, we may bring the same leg to bear a little more against the horse's body, to send him out again. It is very much a question of weight down and weight against, but finely juggled.

Bend on a circle is much improved by maintaining weight into the inside stirrup while bringing a little more lateral pressure to bear against the horse's side at the same time. Clearly, the (unseen) outside leg assists the horse behind the girth.

This simple exercise will be backed up by the outside leg moving behind the girth to support the bend and prevent the horse from escaping onto a new track.

Crookedness

I believe there would be far fewer crooked horses and far fewer crooked riders if people could be made more aware of the almost magical powers of the rider's inside leg. It is such an essential aid that its understanding and practice should be part of everyone's 'equipment'. And therein lies the problem. Since most people are one-sided, they may obtain good results on one rein, but on the other their horse may be crooked. Not because they have done too little – the problem is often quite the contrary. They are crooked because they have done too much.

Above *Most riders find it easier to bend their horse on the left rein as it is generally easier to drop their weight to this side.*

Right *The rider must keep the inside hip forward to support the inside leg. Any leaning will be reflected by the horse, but the rider can correct this by placing more weight into the outside stirrup.*

'Doing too much with the right hand' is a common complaint from many trainers about their students (and many students about themselves) – but they seem unable to correct it. It tends to make their horse easier to ride and bend on the left rein, although a weak left leg may allow the horse to fall in, as seen above. A moment later, this situation was corrected.

Editorial note: What is said here is, of course, statistically true, because the majority of people are right-handed/sided. However, the 'mirror image' effect may be seen in people who are left-handed/sided. Therefore, ultimately, the issue is of one-sided dominance. For the purposes of illustration in this chapter, I have cited examples referring to the more common right-sided issue, but left-handed readers may find that the exact opposite applies to them. If that applies to you, please 'reverse' the examples given.

From years of teaching experience, I believe this most common fault starts below the belt. It concerns the rider's right leg. Overuse of the leg causes an imbalance in the seat which, in turn, forces the rider to overuse the right hand. Instead of making the horse more supple to the right, it generally does the opposite. This is particularly noticeable in turns and circles.

How not to turn right. This shows overuse of the right leg and right rein – a common sight.

'Too much right hand'

'Right-handed dominance' can be much improved by the teacher asking the rider to hold both reins in the left hand for a reasonable period of time. But that only works up to a point. Unfortunately, it is much harder to correct the overuse of the right leg than the underuse. The former can be helped by removing the right stirrup and teaching the rider to let the offending leg hang down. Even then things can go wrong, since the rider's right thigh muscles may overcompensate.

Either way, what generally happens is that the horse wants to move away from the sideways pressure of the rider's right leg. He will then try to move left despite the fact that the rider's hand is asking him to move right. What few appreciate is that the right leg has slightly 'shortened' or contracted and even though the rider's stirrups may look the same length, the horse is pressured by it.

Nine out of ten riders tend to over-aid with the right leg to turn. Instead of moving into pressure this has the result of pushing the horse away, with the rider slipping to the outside.

This misunderstanding or misinterpretation of the situation is compounded further when the rider asks for more bend to the inside. This often causes riders to twist so, if it hasn't already happened, further attempts to flex the horse right simply push the horse further left.

Problem-solving

The only way to cure this very typical scenario is to persuade the rider to advance the inside hip, sit a little more into the inside seatbone and think of letting their weight 'drop' into the inside leg. The rider may then bring the outside rein and leg to bear against the horse as an indirect aid, such as is used in formal Western riding.

The worst thing the rider can do is ask for more bend with the right rein, ask for more bend at the girth with the right leg and turn the upper body too much to the right.

Bad habits do not develop overnight; it can take years to get to a scenario where, as well as the horse being crooked, the rider is too. Worse is to follow – crookedness in the rider generally leads to a state of one leg becoming over-dominant. Then, whatever horse this rider is on, instead of inviting him to turn around the rider's leg and step under the rider's weight, this leg is fighting this intention by pushing him away from it.

Left *Here, the rider corrects herself by transferring more weight to the inside stirrup and immediately the horse moves into the pressure.*

Below *Generally we must think of turning the whole horse when we ride, rather than pulling the head round. The outside rein is essential to the process.*

Muscle memory

It is more difficult to correct a habitual fault than one that is random and simply the result of a momentary imbalance. Often, the more riders try to correct, the worse the fault becomes. There is no easy way to reduce the pressure of the dominant leg other than being aware of it and constantly trying to let it drop – let it go – weight down.

When students first have a lesson on my schoolmaster and I ask them to turn right off the track at say B or E, the riders with 'leg problems' almost always disappear up the school. They are so tight with the right leg, they push the horse sideways and away.

Generally, they end up at the top of the school in a vague sort of shoulder-in movement. When I am asked, 'Why did he do that?' my answer is inevitably the same: 'Because you asked him to.' Many of them had no idea they had one leg much stronger than the other.

By the time they have learned to let go of the dominant leg when it is on the inside (this may take weeks or months) riders often discover they are now less reliant on the same-side rein too.

This is good example of a guest student being able to let go with the unseen right leg and concentrate on the aids of the outside rein and outside leg to turn the horse.

The horse should be gently flexing into the inside rein, with the outside rein applying sideways pressure against the neck.

At the beginning of the turn, the rider weights the inside (unseen) stirrup and moves the horse away from pressure with the outside rein and outside leg in order to move right.

The rider continues to apply sideways pressure from the outside leg as the horse comes round.

The moment the horse straightens, the new inside leg drops to the girth and both legs apply a quick forward aid.

A typical case of cause and effect. It is rewarding to be told by riders that this simple lesson has helped their own horses enormously, but it does take time and patience.

Turns

We are all generally taught the turn on the forehand in our early riding lessons, but too many riders continue with this exercise right through their riding lives and it tends to reinforce bad habits. That is very sad for their horses.

Turning on the forehand in movement places the horse in an unnatural balance, different from the one that he would naturally adopt in freedom. Unfortunately, it is all too easy to focus on the front end instead of riding the whole horse. The tendency in many riding schools is to allow the pupil to pull the horse's head and neck around so that the body can follow. This is putting the cart before the horse. It places the horse firmly on the forehand and causes the quarters to swing out.

By contrast, one of the best exercises to teach rider and horse together and to use gravity and proprioception to their advantage is the turn on the hocks.

Turn on the hocks (*see* left)

Both in movement and from the standstill, the horse will naturally move off from behind. Turning from the hocks or hindquarters, he can take his weight back, engage his hindquarters and push himself around. Once accomplished, the forehand lightens, the forelegs are relieved of their burden and he is free to move in whatever direction he wants.

The aids are relatively simple. The rider sits square, feels gently on the inside rein, and applies a little downward pressure into the inside seatbone and inside stirrup. The inside leg should never be clamped on, instead it hangs roughly vertical – toe at the girth. This allows the horse to bend and move into the rider's weight.

The downward weight aid is then complemented by the rider's outside leg and outside rein, which move against the horse's body (sideways pressure) to turn him into the required direction. Pushing down with the heel is counterproductive, but a little more pressure into the ball of the foot is helpful. This, in turn, allows the horse greater freedom to move into and around the rider's inside leg. I have discovered very few teachers emphasise this point to students, which is a great pity.

This is how we ought to ride horses – doing something that is natural for them. Instead, most riders focus on the front end and think it necessary to pull the head and neck around so that the body can follow. This places the horse firmly on the forehand and might be compared to us going through a door head first, rather than allowing our legs to carry us there.

Anchored

Some riders prefer not to use the stirrups at all to indicate the weight aids. Many rely on transferring the correct feeling through the seatbones, which is equally subtle. There is always the risk, however, that teaching the seat aids to a fairly novice rider may make them tip to the right or left, which is the worst scenario since it causes them to compensate by throwing their weight in the opposite direction. So, for the purposes of this book, I will generally refer to both the seat aids and the weight aids of the feet in the stirrups.

Once we have mastered the turn on the hocks and developed a feel for it, we will begin to appreciate the correct role of our inside leg. It will no longer be the leg that pushes at the horse – it will be his anchor! We will achieve far more bend and suppleness on circles, serpentines and that important entry down the centre line, when we can let it go!

Keeping our weight down is often helped by imagery. When I train riders who have a tendency to draw up with the inside leg, the idea of an anchor seems really to help.

105

Dropping the inside leg and applying a little more pressure into the inside stirrup at the girth is like putting the icing on the cake. If our horse is a little wobbly on a straight line, or hesitant in his turns, deepening our weight into the relevant stirrup will steady and straighten him.

If we wish to make a sudden change of rein, we will have instant obedience by pressing on the inside stirrup to leave the track and turn or move onto the diagonal.

If we want a good canter transition, it is an almost fail-safe way of ensuring that we will get the correct lead. The more we wish to continue the canter, the more we reinforce the weight aid of the inside leg, while the outside leg remains behind the girth. Every horse is different, but generally it is the inside leg aid that makes the horse *want* to canter on the correct lead. Basically, he just follows weight – *see* Chapter 8.

Our pillar of support

The old Masters always referred to the inside leg as a pillar of support. Pillars don't move, so this is a good analogy and one that every student can understand. A good instructor should explain about the importance of the 'feel' of the inside leg, as well as what it does or doesn't do. Most people do too much with it and if only they were taught about weight aids, they might be less inclined to move it forward or back when not appropriate.

As in all riding, just a few inches forward or back can make all the difference. When the inside leg is too far forward it may block the inside shoulder of a sensitive horse; placed too far back it becomes ineffectual as a support and, worse, allows the horse to fall in on the inside shoulder. In both cases, bend will be lost and the horse may drift onto the forehand.

Here again is where my Weight Aid Workshops are so valuable. I invite a couple of students to skip (on the same leg) around the room and ask the others to listen. When I ask the question, 'Where was their weight?' generally, the hands shoot up and they say 'The inside'. Those giving this answer are of course right. The inside leg never blocks the horse. It is the stepping-down leg, which leads him into the various movements. It invites the canter, invites the turn and tells the horse in what direction we wish to go. It is also the leg that gives support to the horse in a bend or a turn. It is indeed a wonderful aid.

Refining the circle

As an example, the 20m or 15m circle to the right in walk, trot or canter will be much improved when we place a little more pressure into the inside (right) stirrup. This is a very useful weight aid as it draws the horse into the correct bend whilst supporting him through its position at the girth. Maintaining the same weight aid for the duration of the circle ensures continuity, but it must be very subtle. In the meantime, we must not forget to maintain the activity of the hocks and prevent the quarters from straying out with the outside leg, placed just behind the girth.

Opposite *The smaller the circle, the more bend. This requires more weight into the inside stirrup as the outside rein moves against the neck to guide the horse into the bend.*

On the larger circle, the inside leg continues to support at the girth, but with less pressure than on the smaller circle.

To make the circle smaller still — say a 10m — we may need to apply more downward pressure. There should be no need to use more inside rein — often quite the contrary. The simple solution is to weight the inside stirrup a little more and bring the outside rein closer to the horse's neck to support. Next time you watch a canter pirouette, notice the effect of the rider's inside leg weighting the stirrup. This is simply taking the movement to a more extreme form.

The tighter the circle, the more the horse is inclined to lean in. Again, the inside leg must support the horse and the rider's body should keep aligned to the horse at all times.

To enlarge the circle, we can again use downward pressure – only this time, it will be into the outside stirrup. This weight aid is rarely taught yet it is wonderfully effective. The inside leg continues to support at the girth; the outside behind. The position remains as before; it is just the 'feel' that will change.

The use of the stirrups to change the rein, or ride a serpentine or a turn is a wonderful aid. The horse should remain bent to the inside (as normal) whichever rein he is on, but by using these weight aids we are able to rely less and less on our hands. Whichever direction we choose, our aiding becomes so imperceptible that this weight aid constitutes an invisible aid – it is so effective.

It was La Guérinière who wrote, 'The weight aid of the stirrups is the finest of all the aids.' I would say ' Amen!' to that, especially as I have found it works with all horses, trained or untrained. ■

In the circle the horse should appear to be evenly bent from head to tail.

8 Moving Away From Pressure

Inside Leg to Outside Hand, Turn on the Hocks and Lateral Work

Riding 'out' to the corner is a very important discipline. The rider gently weights the inside seatbone, while the inside leg maintains impulsion and bend.

Applying sideways pressure against the horse to move him out or away from the leg is, in many ways, simpler than asking the horse to move into pressure and around our leg. Every time we groom a horse and move him around in the stable, we will be using sideways pressure. In this case, it will be our hand that applies weight against the horse. 'Move over here, move over there!' ... and so on.

The horse generally responds to any 'sideways pressure' placed against his body, by moving away in the opposite direction. In the seventeenth century, a group of master horsemen developed this natural reaction into a specific movement. The shoulder-in is of great benefit to suppleness, balance and engagement.

Once mounted, the idea of placing sideways pressure against the horse is not dissimilar. Generally, this is what happens when we talk about 'applying an aid'. For the purposes of clarity, I shall be referring to this pressing action as '*weight against*' rather than '*weight down*' as described in the previous chapter.

These 'weight against' aids can be enormously helpful – as in turning away, moving sideways, staying out and so on – they can also be extremely disrupting when ignorantly applied. Just as important as knowing when to apply pressure is to know when *not to* and when to take it off.

First – balance in all things

Clearly, our upper body, supported by our back, is essential to the distribution of our weight in the saddle. If we don't sit up, we can't let our weight down. Neither can we use our legs in a free and functional way. To sit up correctly requires a supple back protected by strong core muscles and it is a mistake to think of relaxing the stomach muscles when, in fact, we need to stretch and advance them.

By contrast, the seat muscles, which have to form a base for the rider, should be relaxed and able to spread outward so that we are sitting on a broad-based surface. Tight gluteals will tend to drive the horse away from the pressure and a hard seat is neither a comfortable nor safe seat.

Freedom to go forward

No horse enjoys his rider hugging him with the legs, but the legs are our most important aids for the different signals and commands we need to make. Working together with the seat aids, they have the power to change direction, gait, balance and movement.

The trick in the giving of any request is to ask and then allow. There should be a moment of 'on' and a moment of 'off'. If we are not passive in between times, the signals we give with our legs and seat will become meaningless. We need to give the horse time to feel, hear and act.

'Inside leg to outside hand'

We have already discussed moving the horse inward – i.e. away from the outside leg, as in the turn on the hocks. It is time, therefore, to think about moving the horse outwards away from the inside leg. Most riders know and understand the concept of riding 'out to the track', but how many do this correctly? For the most part, even quite experienced riders may focus on the front end of the horse when they should be thinking about taking the horse out from the middle. This ensures that the horse is still looking to the inside of the school, which requires a degree of bend. Why is this so important? Basically, we simply cannot negotiate the perimeters of the school correctly unless the horse is looking and bent to the inside, whichever rein he is on.

Since the tendency with almost any horse will be to 'fall in', achieving correct bend will be the role of the inside leg applying sideways pressure to stay out, but only as much as is required.

Above Straightness! The result of all our bending work to date. Without the one, we don't have the other.

Right Always ride out to the track with inside bend.

The expression 'inside leg to outside hand' is therefore very helpful, provided we remember to open the outside hand so the horse is able to respond correctly and move away from pressure. The moment he arrives at the wall we should automatically release the pressure of the leg while the hand gives forward again.

Bend at all times

Unfortunately, most riders only appear to think about bend when it comes to riding circles or starting lateral work. This is not enough. Simply to negotiate the school correctly, there has to be presence of bend throughout the horse's body at all times, especially if he is to look and flex to the inside. With corners to be negotiated constantly, the only time he should be dead straight will be on the diagonal, in a turn across the school for the few strides

A horse who is deemed to be really straight in an arena is one who is very slightly flexed to the inside. In this way the quarters — which are wider — can then line up correctly with the forehand.

after he has completed the turn off the long side (until he commences the next one) or coming down the centre line. Even then he must be prepared with the correct bend well in advance of his destination point.

Without inside flexion, the horse will tend to fall in on the inside shoulder when ridden on the track despite the best efforts of the rider to keep him straight.

As the work becomes more demanding, so does the need for greater flexibility. This seems to be the most difficult thing for students to take on board, which would explain why so few riders go deep into their corners or ride figure work with a horse who is truly ambidextrous (equal on both reins).

Generally, as already mentioned, the horse will have a stiff side and a more flexible side. Like us, the majority of horses will find one way of moving much easier than on the opposite rein. One-sidedness may well

have been exacerbated by our own failures, but awareness about it can be greatly helped when we introduce lateral work. The normal practice in the first of these lateral movements depends upon sideways pressure from the inside leg.

The leg-yield is a good example of this concept. We bend the horse as though about to ride a circle and then put pressure against his side to move him outwards and away from the circle – usually diagonally across the school. Again, the inside leg moves against the horse while the outside rein should open quietly, to allow this.

Every step of the circle must involve good bend and stretch so it is important to allow sufficiently with the outside hand for the horse to fill the rein.

Here, the rider turns the upper body and applies sideways pressure with the inside leg to ask for leg-yield on the circle. Again, the rider should sit slightly into the inside seatbone.

Every exercise is different, but the one that can cause the greatest confusion to start with is the shoulder-in. It is somehow ironic that this is considered the simplest of the lateral movements, when actually to ride it well it is probably the most sophisticated.

Shoulder-in

Of all the dressage movements, the shoulder-in promotes bend, balance and brilliance.

Shoulder-in was first utilised by the French in the eighteenth century and was pronounced by the English Masters to be a miracle cure for all the horse's weaknesses. It is undoubtedly the best lateral exercise to improve the horse's balance. In teaching the horse to move away from pressure we are using the inside leg predominantly. (Later when we come to ride the half-pass, travers and renvers, we move him away with the outside leg.)

Another anomaly of this movement is that the horse is expected to bend and look forward in one direction, whilst the requirement is to move away and step sideways in the opposite direction. A definite contradiction! For this reason, a rider should be very clear of the aids in their own head before the horse is introduced to the movement.

Weight aids for shoulder-in

Different people have different ideas about the aids for shoulder-in, but for me they have to be logical. For this reason, I start by sitting tall and central and commence the exercise with a small circle – roughly 10m is ideal. This will prepare the horse by bending him to the inside, prior to continuing in that bend for the duration of the shoulder-in.

I am very conscious of the weight aids, and mentally I will ride or teach the movement in two parts. For example in left shoulder-in, I will:

● Bring the forehand off the track so the horse's head and shoulders (and the rider's) are looking left as we proceed to ride the circle. For this, the inside leg will support the horse at the girth and I will employ *downward pressure into the inside (seatbone) and leg*.

● On returning to the track, I ride the first step of a new circle – *downward pressure* – before centralising my weight again. At this point, I now aid the horse's main body to move away from the pressure of my inside leg placed just behind the girth. This is a very different feeling. By applying *sideways pressure with the inside leg* – generally a nudge or gentle tap is the most effective – I am giving the horse a lateral aid.

1–5 Right *Here, we clearly see the significance of the three-track movement. Sitting slightly deeper on the inside seatbone keeps the horse bending left. Placing a little more pressure into the outside stirrup is a useful aid to keep the horse on the track.*

As with all movements that require bend, the rider's outside leg should support the horse by remaining quietly behind the girth.

For students (and horses) new to the movement, it can be challenging to think one moment of riding forward for a single step and then to think 'move sideways', but most students get the gist in the first lesson especially if they can learn from a schoolmaster who already knows the exercise.

The reason for that first step is to invite the horse's head and shoulders to move off the track, before he is asked to move sideways and away from the pressure of the inside leg. Without doing this, there would be no bend in the horse's body, which is essential to the movement .

Here, the rider prepares the horse for the shoulder-in by sitting tall and into the inside seatbone, flexing the horse to the inside.

1–3 Right and Below
By maintaining inside flexion and keeping the rider's inside hip forward, the rider adopts the shoulder-in position to mirror her horse as he moves away from her inside leg along the track.

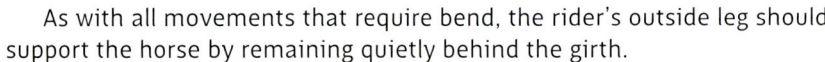

Perfecting the balance

The late Portuguese Master Nuno Oliveira called the shoulder-in the Alpha and Omega of riding. Even with a horse who is never going to do a dressage test in his life, this lateral movement is destined to improve his balance for life. It will teach him to use himself behind correctly, lighten his shoulders, and will make him more supple to the extent, probably, of prolonging his life. Teaching this to a novice horse is much more successful when the rider is sensitive and knows when to ask and – just as important – when to 'let go' for a moment, so the horse can carry out the request. As with every movement and in every phase of every aid, there has to be a moment of

In Portugal, riding the shoulder-in and travers on a circle is very popular. Here, the horse clearly bends and moves to the right with the rider using the weight aid of inside leg for bend.

Riding shoulder-fore as part of a circle is very beneficial to greater engagement behind from the inside hind, and general flexibility.

release – before the aid is applied again. This is far more effective than just pushing him sideways.

'Feel' is all important in our lateral work. Once the horse is looking and bending in the required direction, exactly how we 'move the horse away' depends very much on the horse's sensitivity and character in terms of how much or how little pressure is required. Often, sitting momentarily into the outside seatbone will give the horse the idea for what is required.

Generally, however, some pressure with the inside lower leg or thigh is required to send the horse away. With a younger horse we may need to be more specific. I generally ask with a light touch of the lower leg so he can move his inside hind underneath the body mass one step at a time. Once the horse knows the movement, just the laying on of the asking leg is often enough. That is one of the reasons why it is so important that riders do not grip or hold on all the time.

Too many riders forget that the outside leg is almost as important as the inside one. The rider's outside thigh and knee help support the angle of the shoulder-in, while the lower leg keeps the quarters from swinging out. The shoulder-in requires that the horse remains bent throughout the movement and it is often wise to ride another small circle halfway up the track before continuing.

Travers and half-pass

Head to the wall in the form of travers, and half-pass, require the horse to look and bend into the same direction as the movement, which should be easier than shoulder-in for both horse and rider. Travers is normally ridden up the track, whereas half-pass is generally ridden diagonally across the school. In both cases, we sit slightly deeper into the inside stirrup or seatbone to 'lead' the horse into the required direction. As with all these movements, it is important to sit up and look the same way as the horse, who should be gently flexed to the inside.

If the rider is already familiar with the turn on the hocks, it will make the riding of these two lateral movements so much easier. As with shoulder-in, I will start the exercise of travers with a 10m circle to bend the horse into the required direction and to send him that way too. For example, in travers right, I will:

1. Approach the track at an angle of roughly 35 degrees. Just prior to the horse straightening, I will half-halt with the outside rein while keeping the horse bent to the inside. *Now I must deepen the weight into my right stirrup and my right seatbone* to lead the horse forward and sideways.

2. As with the turn on the hocks, I ask the horse to move right and away from the pressure of my outside (left) leg behind the girth. At the same time my outside rein will bear gently against the horse's neck while the horse looks and flexes to the inside. Keeping the inside hip forward and *gently weighting the inside stirrup* gives the horse his pillar of support, which is so important in all lateral movements.

When it comes to moving into half-pass, the aids are exactly the same as for the travers, only it is generally ridden diagonally across the school. In all these lateral movements, too many riders forget that the outside

Start the travers with a 10m circle: the last step of the circle will be your first step into travers as you approach the track at an angle. You should stay central throughout.

leg is just as important as the inside one. The rider's outside thigh and knee help support the angle of the different movements, while the lower leg applies pressure into the inside stirrup to maintain bend. Both the shoulder-in and the travers require the horse to remain bent throughout the movement and it is often wise to ride another small circle halfway up the track before continuing.

Moving out

By now, the phrase 'moving away from pressure' should be very clear to anyone. It is used again and again in dressage lessons, especially when

Sequence right *A good way to correct right-leg dominance is to ride travers down the track, where the inside hip is advanced and the inside leg naturally provides a 'pillar' for bend.*

Left *Half-pass can be ridden in walk, trot and canter. With a soft inside rein, the rider bends the horse in the direction of travel. The rider advances the inside hip and deepens their weight into the inside stirrup and seatbone. The horse moves into and around the inside leg, encouraged by the outside leg, which applies sideways pressure just behind the girth.*

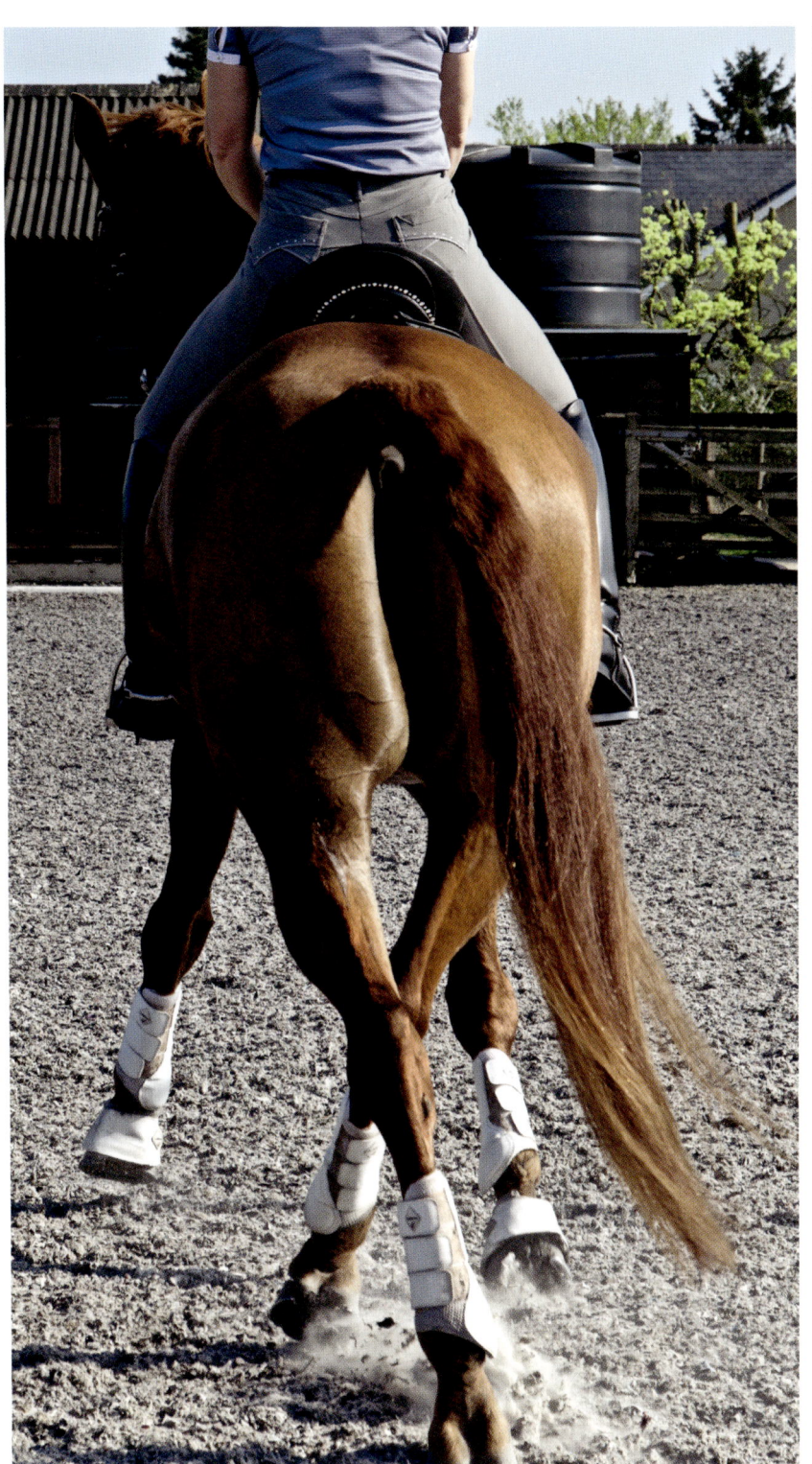

Left and next page
Half-pass with very good crossing of legs and the horse bending correctly into the direction of travel. The rider's inside weight aid is at the girth, while the outside leg is guiding the outside hind under and through.

the rider is being introduced to lateral work. But long before we do this, we will have been using these aids quite naturally to turn or help move the horse around the school without thinking about it – for example, circles and serpentines, keeping the horse out to the track and so on. Clearly, riding 'inside leg to outside hand' is nothing new.

Never forget that the seat aids must at all times mimic the weight aids of the stirrups. Movements into pressure or away from pressure – as discussed in Chapter 6 – should always complement each other. Nowhere is this more apparent than in the lateral movements.

Weighting the outside stirrup in shoulder-in is another very useful example of using downward pressure to complement the application of sideways pressure from the inside leg.

Protecting the horse

Once we are more aware of the weight aids and how they govern the horse's balance and way of going, we should notice a much heightened sense of communication between us. Basically, we will be asking less with our hands, while even our seat and legs should be quieter as the horse submits to the natural sources to which we are now allowing him to respond. Nobody has trained him to understand these matters … it is all absolutely as it should be. There need be no prodding, pushing or pulling of reins – simply an indication from our own bodyweight. ■

A good example of travers left. Here my horse looks, bends and moves into the downward pressure of my inside leg,

9 Jumping into Canter
Leading the Horse to Lead Himself

There has to be an energy within the rider to initiate the canter strike-off if it is to be upward and instant. We lighten our weight on the back of the saddle to enable the horse to push off the outside hind.

Of all the movements, it is always the canter that seems to throw up the most problems for students and their horses. Whether this is because the gait is generally speedier, or horses tend to misbehave because the rider is less balanced, it is hard to tell. I suspect it is a mixture of both.

Generally, I find it is a lack of knowledge about the weight aids that can spoil the canter. Most people know the inside leg should be at the girth, the outside leg behind the girth, but it is the 'feel' that is everything – both in riding the canter and teaching it – and this is not discussed enough.

But first, let us put ourselves in the horse's shoes. We have to appreciate that he needs as much freedom as possible to push off with the outside hind in order to take up the correct lead, and this should inform us where our weight needs to be.

Above *This is a nice collected canter, with the horse looking forward and clearly pushing off from the outside hind. The rider's inside leg sits at the girth and the inside rein should be light to accommodate the incoming inside fore.*

Left *In the downward phase of canter, it is important for the rider to sit up to maintain balance. Here you can clearly see the position of both legs.*

With a school to negotiate, there is always the danger that the rider will force the horse to go disunited or change legs, not because he wants to, but because he has no choice. Too much movement in the rider's body can be very unsettling for the horse, and to continue on the correct lead in a constricted area where corners are continually coming up would make any horse feel threatened. It is a miracle that most generally manage as well as they do.

Canter transitions

A good canter transition is all down to timing and 'feel'. The horse cannot push off from the outside hind if the rider sits too much into the back of the saddle. Unless he is very big and strong, the horse will feel blocked by the seat and, since the rider's weight often drifts to the outside on a corner or circle, he will be doubly compromised.

Lightening the seat further to accommodate the horse's upward movement.

Instead, the rider should advance their inside hip and sit into the inside seatbone. This will free up the outside leg and lighten the outside seatbone so the horse has a chance to step under more easily and push off behind in every stride.

Often, people find it hard to think about their hips. What will really help the horse is the act of deepening the inside leg and putting more weight into the inside stirrup. The feeling should be one of stepping down – never pushing against.

On the ground, this is exactly what would happen if we cantered or skipped ourselves – which is where, again, my Weight Aid Workshops are so valuable. In order to push off from behind, we have to jump into the inside leading leg and that is the feeling I try to teach riders. 'Think of skipping right!' (Or left, as appropriate.)

It is the same on the horse, once we let our weight down and step into the inside stirrup, we can push off more effectively with the outside leg behind the girth and the horse can follow our lead. Provided we keep our weight directly under us and let our weight go down naturally through gravity, our canter will be confirmed.

There is no reason for it to be lost, or for the horse to go disunited or change, just as long as we maintain pressure in that inside stirrup. It is also important that the outside hand does not give away too much, which can throw the horse onto the inside shoulder, instead of keeping his inside hind well under him.

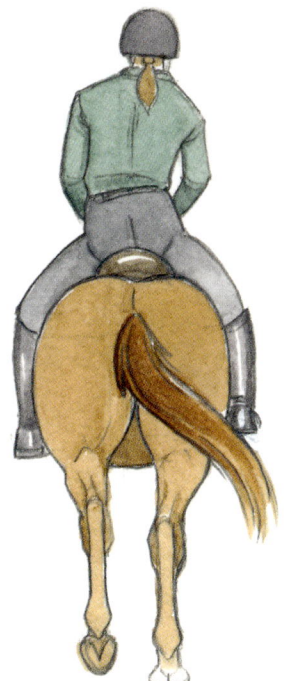

An excellent example of seat in the middle of the saddle, knees down and pressure on the inside stirrup – so important for the canter transition.

By leaning into the required canter lead, the rider is actually confusing the horse as their weight will tend to slide to the outside instead of remaining over the horse's leading leg.

Counter-canter

Once riders have tuned into the feeling of canter through their feet, it is easier to connect with the mirror effect on their seatbones. More weight in the inside stirrup means more weight into the inside seatbone* to complement it – but at all times sit up. Remind yourself of the old maxim, what goes up must come down.

For many riders, counter-canter seems scary – a real challenge – but once you understand that your inside leg is going to take care of everything, all you have to do is believe. So, ride a 20m circle at the end of the school and then take the diagonal across the school to change the rein and just concentrate on keeping your weight into the original (now the outside) leg. Keep pressing down on the outside stirrup and ride up the track in counter-canter without changing a thing.

Before commencing counter-canter, always ride a circle to improve suppleness and bend, keeping your weight slightly more to the inside.

Editorial note: Traditionally 'inside' and 'outside' refer to the bend of the horse, rather than the geography of the school. However, whereas in most circumstances the horse's inside bend will be to the inside of the school, this is not the case in counter-canter. Therefore, in this section, to assist the description of the movement, I am referring to 'inside' and 'outside' in terms of the school.

It is essential that you still continue to look over the horse's leading leg (now the leg to the outside of the school). Your original 'inside' leg is now to the 'outside' of the horse to support the bend which, again, is correct.

As for your original outside (now the inside) hand – this must still check or half-halt on the rein. You are still looking to the outside of the school, as is the horse. When you have succeeded in riding a few steps of counter-canter in this way, you will wonder why you ever thought it difficult. No one has told the horse he is on the 'wrong' leg. Just let him know he did the right thing when you finish. And never be greedy – return to trot before the next corner, when things might go wrong.

Of all the weight aids, I have probably had more success with students discovering these feelings in counter-canter than any other movement. At the start of the lesson, I remind them that the weight of a human head is around 12–14lb and that if they move it the wrong way, it's a serious weight aid. Only change it when you have finished the counter-canter and returned to trot. It's important the horse knows you both did the right thing.

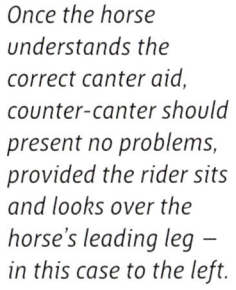

Once the horse understands the correct canter aid, counter-canter should present no problems, provided the rider sits and looks over the horse's leading leg – in this case to the left.

Canter half-pass

Back into normal canter, riding the half-pass is surprisingly uncomplicated. In many ways, it is much easier than walk or trot half-pass (*see* Chapter 8), since the horse is not crossing his legs, but jumping forwards and sideways. At a later stage you can use the same aids and the same feeling to introduce the half-pass in the other gaits, after you have perfected your shoulder-in.

Riding the canter half-pass is one of those movements where everything you do in a normal canter is simply highlighted in the lateral work. The most important thing is to maintain a feeling of weight into the inside stirrup as you would for a circle but, instead of turning your body, you simply continue up the school forwards and sideways. This is the one

Canter half-pass left requires the rider to sit into the left seatbone, with a good inside leg position to support the horse at the girth for bend and direction. The outside rein guides the forehand left; the outside leg moves the horse sideways away from the pressure behind the girth.

movement that probably relies on your inside hip more than anything.

By maintaining the canter aid — inside leg on girth, outside leg behind — you start the half-pass sitting slightly deeper into the inside seatbone. The horse should remain bent around the inside leg as you apply more weight into the inside stirrup. This invites the horse to travel forward and sideways.

Hips and shoulders rule

The most important aid in canter half-pass must surely be that of the rider's inside hip. By keeping the inside seatbone forward and slightly weighted, you can better support the inside leg at the girth. As with all the

Canter half-pass right requires the rider to advance the inside hip and apply more weight into the inside stirrup. Both horse and rider are looking right and the horse bends gently around the inside leg at the girth.

weight aids, putting a little more pressure into the inside stirrup will draw the horse into the direction of travel. The secret to a good half-pass is for the rider to keep the ribcage open and tall, particularly to the inside.

The rider's shoulders should remain level, but it is all too easy to let the inside one drop as the partnership begins to move right or left. It definitely helps to think of having an extra rib to the inside to prevent this from happening, and remembering that any twisting or drooping of the upper body will denigrate the sideways movement.

The horse must look into the direction of the half-pass, not so much by bending his neck to the inside, but by bending through the girth and through the poll. He should look ahead, slightly flexed into the direction of travel, and it is important that the rider looks the same way and keeps the inside rein soft.

The outside rein acts as a counter-balance to the movement, and acts against the horse's neck by pressing slightly sideways. Don't forget that the rein aids used in this way are generally recognised as pressure aids themselves. To complement the outside rein, the rider's outside leg is now applied behind the girth to nudge the quarters across.

It is very important that the quarters do not precede the forehand in the half-pass but, provided the rider's inside leg is deep and the rider leads from the inside hip, with a tall, supportive upper body, all should be well.

Change of leg

I have always recommended teaching the horse changes out of counter-canter but before we discuss this, let us outline the basic aids for a flying change across the diagonal.

The rider leaves the track on the normal lead (we will assume left in this example). We start on the left rein with slightly more weight on the inside (left) stirrup and seatbone. We are looking over the horse's leading (left) leg. The right rein supports the horse to the outside. To change, we neutralise the rein aids before transferring our weight into the right stirrup and right seatbone. At the same time we gently check on the new outside rein (left). The rider should sit central and now be looking over the new leading leg (right).

The key factor will be the change of weight through the seatbones and how we use our stirrups. In counter-canter, we will have been bending the horse slightly to the outside of the school (see note under Counter-canter), sitting into the outside seatbone, which will be in advance of the inside, and applying more pressure into the outside stirrup poised at the girth. (For example in counter-canter on the right rein, the rider will be sitting slightly left, the left leg is positioned at the girth and the right leg will be behind the girth.)

Having navigated the school in this way, we can then ask the horse for a change by reversing the aids back to normal after coming out of a corner. Do not think of bending one way and then another; think of releasing the horse from the left bend and allowing him to move straight again.

During the flying change, the rider should sit as centrally as possible, the main emphasis being the change of weight through the seatbones and stirrups (see text).

The most difficult thing will be the synchronicity of your aids. From stepping down and keeping that feeling to the outside in counter-canter, now think of straightening the horse's neck and concentrate on the feeling of stepping down into the new (original) leading leg — the leg that would normally be the inside leg on a circle or circuit of the school.

This stepping down feeling would be much improved by 'playing horses' on the ground. Practise being a horse and leading first with one leg, and then pushing off and skipping into the opposite one. Then try the exercise the other way round. You may think that experimenting with these aids on your own two feet is laughable; I would argue that it is laudable. It really improves your sense of 'feel' and, best of all, in the counter-canter work, it improves your timing.

Cantering straight down the centre line will have been much improved after all the bend and lateral work.

Always finish the canter work with a joyous, forward and 'normal' canter around the whole school. ■

Of all the movements, the canter requires the most balanced position from the rider. If the inside leg does not provide a 'pillar' of support it will be hard to maintain bend or an 'uphill' movement. The rider must also keep the inside hip forward at all times to mirror the horse.

10 Onward and Upward
The Three Ps – Piaffe, Passage and Pirouette

This is a good example of the horse bringing his weight back – with the hocks well underneath in order to lighten the forehand. The rider sits in the centre of the saddle with the inside leg at the girth asking for lift.

Collection is a word that can so often be misinterpreted, but the main idea is to have the horse more together, more instantly on the aids and in a position to give the rider exactly what is requested.

This requires that the horse is in good balance, with the hocks placed well under the quarters and the forehand light. A collected horse should be able to spring into action at a moment's request – for example, walk to canter, rein-back to canter, trot to halt, halt to piaffe and so on.

The energy and weight of the horse should be 'back'; this simply means that the horse is no longer on the forehand as he would be in his early training. Thus, the rider should feel that the balance is behind the saddle, with very little weight in the reins.

It takes many years to train a horse to the state of suppleness and strength in the back and hind limb joints to be able to carry out the more collected movements. For me, collected walk is the first of these, whereby we want shorter and higher steps without spoiling the four-time rhythm of the walk. This should all be achieved without tension on the reins – as taught me in the Portuguese School. Using stronger leg or seat aids is not the answer. Indeed the collection of the walk should feel light and energetic. The aids should reflect this.

In classical circles, riders often talk about 'closing the horse'. This simply means bringing the hind legs further underneath before commencing the piaffe. Sitting as tall as possible, we bring both legs back to gather the hind legs of the horse. Our weight is now above the horse's strongest point.

When teaching the higher airs, I am always most concerned about the rider's weight. Sitting too heavily will certainly not invite the horse to lift his back and, as a consequence, there can be no meaningful lift through the forehand. Blocking the horse in front with too much contact will make the movements cumbersome and earth-bound.

With the correct weight aids, however, the horse should feel 'shorter and rounder' throughout and there should be no difficulty in ensuring that the poll remains the highest point.

Top riders know very well that however strong their horse may be, finding the optimum place to sit is essential. Here we see a good example of the three-point seat with all the weight of the rider remaining over the horse's centre of balance in this very correct passage.

The three-point seat again

Almost the first thing upon which I focus when teaching these higher movements to riders new to this work is the position of the rider's seat and legs. How the latter are applied determines the weight and 'feel' of their seat in the saddle and can make all the difference to the quality of each movement or exercise requested. For example, in the rein-back, with the rider sitting deeper on the front of the saddle, the very act of moving both thighs back helps free the horse's back. This can make the horse much more willing and able to step back without hollowing or resisting.

Once he is unencumbered by our weight, a really well-schooled horse will draw his hocks under his body once given the freedom to do so. From this position, we can then teach him the first steps of piaffe.

Piaffe

It is often easier to teach piaffe by using the rein-back as a launch-pad. Using the aids described in Chapter 6, we ask the horse for two or three steps backward and then think forward again – but only in baby steps. This is done by gently giving and taking with the legs and fingers. No one can tell you how much to give and how much to take or, indeed, how to resist – we have to feel it for ourselves.

So, incrementally, we allow the horse forward. Just as we learn how to halt and then go forward again without thinking about it very much, we use similar aids. Thus, with a feeling of collection throughout, we begin to govern each and every forward step. Just thinking 'piaffe' can be very beneficial.

As noted earlier, moving our legs back has two effects.

1. It places us more on the twist or front of the saddle, which will gently block the forward movement and put the horse on the spot.

2. It allows us the freedom with the legs to 'scoop the horse up' and forward and 'under us' by energising him behind.

In piaffe, the rider sits tall and moves his legs slightly back to gather his horse's hocks more under him. The rein is light and he sits towards the front of the saddle to free the horse's back.

141

To obtain a balanced piaffe with the majority of the weight of the horse on his hocks, the rider needs to sit as tall and as close to the pommel as possible.

During the first of these lessons, the horse should be allowed to step forward if required. The idea is to reduce the steps little by little until the horse is strong enough behind to take more weight on his hocks and raise his legs diagonally on the spot.

Once the horse is truly engaged, his hind legs may reach right under the rider's stirrups – but this often depends upon conformation and type. It is important always to ask for activity, so the forehand can rise up light and expressive. An 'uphill' action is not sufficiently seen in competition dressage, where the piaffes can be earthbound, flat and very disappointing indeed. Too often we see the hind end raised, instead of the forehand, which does not comply with FEI rules.

This picture demonstrates how tall the rider should sit to alleviate the horse's back from pressure in this very upward movement.

The best piaffes are generally those that emerge as a result of the rider remaining very centred. By bringing our knees more under ourselves, we can invite the horse's hind legs to lift and step up and under. The more we make room for all this to happen, the more the horse can 'round'. The horse must never be *forced* to bring his weight back – it should happen naturally as a result of increased engagement behind.

Passage

The passage is a wonderful movement to teach both horse and rider together, as it gives riders a great feeling of lift and achievement. By

In passage, I deepen my knees and bring my lower legs back behind the girth to 'scoop' the horse's hind legs up and under him. By raising my own centre of gravity, I can feel my horse lifting through the forehand in response. This is an extreme form of collection but note how raised and arched forward the neck should be. By allowing more, the horse can 'grow'!

collecting the horse more and more through sitting tall and inviting him to remain on the bit through gentle, asking fingers, the rider achieves greater flexion through the poll and jaw. This has a reflex effect on the horse's back, quarters and hind legs.

The rider may now start to bring both of their own legs further behind the girth. This action – as with the piaffe – steadies the gait and places the rider's weight more over the front of the saddle. Once this is achieved, there is a great sense of liberation to the horse, whose back is now relieved of pressure where normally the weight of the rider would inhibit any desire to lift up more readily.

Once the rider is balanced in this way, it is easier to open the hips and to slide the legs back to 'pick up' the horse. Here, the rider is supported by the twist, which makes it possible to move back the whole of the legs, not just from the knees downward.

This is another example of a happy forward passage with no resistance from Prazer.

Sometimes it helps the horse if we adopt a slightly more forward position in the passage. The main objective in these advanced movements is always to give the horse space and freedom to elevate as much as possible.

Here I demonstrate the passage, riding one-handed and holding my stick, as one might a sword in the time-honoured way of yesteryear. By staying over the horse's centre of balance i.e. just behind the withers, my horse elevates throughout his body, with the poll as the highest point.

Now the rider is in a position to 'scoop' the horse upward and forward without in any way inhibiting his back. One of the greatest difficulties for people who are not taught the seat aids in this way is a tendency merely to send the horse forward, but without any lift.

Once the first few steps of passage are taken, the horse begins to enjoy the sensation of elevation. It is very important that, at this early stage, the rider does not suddenly descend back into the normal sitting position. Instead, our human posture makes it possible to lift up too. We can raise our own centre of gravity by stretching or extending our front line, which really supports what is required of the horse. By this stage of training, the horse is usually desirous of coming with us in all that we do. It is a wonderful sensation when two partners can come together in this way.

Canter pirouette

Once a rider has attained a feeling for collection in all gaits, and the canter work to date has been successful, riding canter pirouette is a very rewarding progression from the canter half-pass. The aids will be practically the same — the horse is moving and bending sideways into the rider's leading leg and, to make the turn, it is mainly a question of half-halting. It would be a mistake

Charlotte demonstrating the whole ethos of taking the horse's weight back to liberate the forehand. Note the upright seat over the horse's centre of balance, depth of the rider's thigh and knee and the weight aid of the inside leg.

Prazer, at 22 years of age, still manages to transfer his weight back in the canter pirouette. My most important aid is the inside leg, coupled with being centred over his strongest point.

to think this is done with the outside rein alone. A proper half-halt requires real balance, and particularly relies on good upward core strength, which allows the rider to concentrate and deepen their weight without pushing down against the horse's back.

Instead, the focus for the rider's weight is directed through the strongest part of the horse's back as the rider deepens the thighs and knees to cement the sensation of remaining on the spot. All this is assisted by the outside rein, which moves against the outside of the horse's neck as the rider thinks *into* the turn.

Here again an understanding of the weight aids is essential. The rider must never collapse the upper body to 'help' the horse as is too often seen. On the contrary, by sitting tall to the inside (I always ask my students to imagine they have an extra rib on the side to which they will move) the rider is much better able to deepen the inside leg and seatbone and invite the horse into the turn.

For those riders who are familiar with the half-pirouette in walk, the feeling will be very similar. Even in canter, it is not at all a question of more inside rein. The horse should be flexed into the movement, but that is all – there should be little or no weight in the rider's inside hand.

The most important aid will be the deepening of the rider's inside seatbone and increased downward pressure into the stirrup. Without a high degree of collection, the canter will be too forward-going to remain on or almost on the spot. This is much assisted by the rider's core strength and ability to lift the ribcage while still thinking forward and round.

It is the aid of the outside rein against the neck that actually dictates the turning away of the forehand. This aid is backed up by the outside leg moving against the horse's body just behind the girth, with an application of our old friend – sideways pressure.

With regard to the inside rein, the canter pirouette is very much a case of 'less is more'. The main instruction comes from the weight aid of the inside leg with a deepening of the leg at the girth, some little pressure on the inside stirrup and – more important than anything perhaps – the feeling of leading the horse up and into the turn. This requires a tall upper body and the inside hip forward, which is an important support aid. It allows the rider's inside leg to drop without blocking the movement and this allows the inside leg to act as a pillar of support to the horse as he bends around it.

In many ways, this is one of the easiest aids to spot, since the horse moves so willingly into the pressure by bending and yielding into the required direction. A beautiful movement if well performed, it is perhaps the ultimate example of the use of weight aids – and arguably the most effective. ■

11 Going with the Flow
The Finishing Touches — the Reins

Although this book is mainly concerned with the weight and pressure aids of the rider's seat and legs, we must never forget that the rein aids must always work in concert with the aids of the body. These should be almost invisible. Indeed, the weight of the rein alone can make a profound difference to the quality of the work we produce.

A nice straight line from bit to elbow — ready for the work ahead.

Hands that speak

There will be times when one rein will open, the other will close. As one allows, the other supports. None of this should involve any obvious movements. Of all the aids, those of the hands should be the most discreet and the feeling of the hand around the rein should be light but clear. The hands should be held as a pair. No matter how much the rider turns or angles their body throughout the different movements, the two hands must remain opposite each other — as though they are in one glove.

The width apart may differ slightly from horse to horse. The old rule about the width of the hands corresponding to the width of the bit is pretty accurate. We will only develop sensitive, feeling fingers when we ride with bent elbows and firm wrists which flow into the hand itself. There should be no break between the wrist and the back of the hand. Always carry the thumbs on top as this helps to develop feeling, sensitive fingers. If the wrists are slack or floppy, there will be no real control of the hands and the horse's mouth will surely suffer.

We can always judge the correct contact by looking at the angle of the horse's head. The correct length of rein will allow the head to be just in front of the vertical, even when the horse is fully collected.

Whilst one hand may ask and the other may give, they should still remain as a pair. The give and take of the fingers allows us the ability to 'speak' to the horse and the inside rein is generally the one that asks for flexion, while the outside tends to support and confirm — whether in a turn or a lateral movement.

Open the way

For most of our forward riding, we should think of our two reins as being 'open' — the width of the bit apart — no more, to provide a clear, unfettered pathway for our horse to move ahead.

As we progress in our understanding of these aids, we will discover that the application of a closed rein, or an indirect rein placed against the horse's neck, will require that we open the other rein. This should be just enough to invite the horse to look or to flex to the right or left — not to turn the whole neck, as is too often seen. Correct flexion affects the way in which the horse moves and balances. These aids must not contradict each other.

Here, we are preparing for passage on the circle. The most important thing is that the horse is gently bent from nose to tail so that the inside rein can be comparatively soft.

Suffice to say that the reins should work in tandem with every other aid. They must complement those of the legs, seat and upper body as described throughout this book.

At all times we must take care not to issue confusing instructions. So, if the legs say forward, the hands must allow. If the seat says stop, the hands must close — but the moment the horse has obeyed, they must open again. If the hands say move left, the legs and our weight must complement them … and so on. In between each command and in whatever we do, we must always return 'to neutral' again.

Quiet contact

First, however, if we are to teach the horse to take his weight back and use himself behind, we must have contact. For this, the horse should be accepting of the bit and happy in his mouth, able to respond to the quietest of fingers by flexing at the poll and through the jaw so that his nose comes towards the vertical. All our work to date should have prepared him for this, since it is important that the hands should never act alone.

Once this is understood, the time should come when we are able to be ride with invisible aids.

There should be no need for overt movements of the hand, except perhaps when we give the rein completely as in the walk on a long rein – when we may take our body forward to allow the horse to stretch fully. Otherwise, the hands should remain quiet.

Nevertheless, there are things going on. The rein aids should be very discreet and, provided the hands remain as a pair at all times, an onlooker should see nothing. A good seat makes for a good pair of hands, but if we are not to pull back, there must always be the sense of giving forward.

A supple but quiet upper body allows for quiet hands. Think of riding 'waist to hands' in all that you do. This encourages you to use your core muscles, which must be supported by a supple back. Generally, the hands should rest (never lean) at the base of the horse's neck or be held just above and in front of the withers. Hands held behind the withers will tend to creep back.

Although much of our work – our use of the school, our circles, turns, transitions and zigzags – require many different weight and leg aids, our

When you give the rein – give the rein!

hands should appear to do very little. If we are riding the horse from behind, there should be no sense of pulling back, as the horse will automatically turn as we do. Instead, the small requests we make with our fingers are simply to ask for downward flexion (on the bit) and lateral flexion – to let the horse look and bend into the new rein. Clearly, these simple requests merely complement the aids of the seat and legs.

There is nothing wrong with allowing your hand to touch the horse's neck. For example, turn left – left (unseen) hand gently opens and 'asks'. Right rein supports by moving indirectly against the horse's neck.

Direct and indirect reins

The more we use the school and ride through the many exercises available to us, the more times there will be when one rein may open, while the other will close. The opening rein is called the direct rein as it directly indicates to the horse the way to go.

By contrast, the rein that supports this action by moving against the horse's neck is called the indirect rein. This name is given because, basically, it is sending the horse in the opposite direction – into the opening rein. The bearing effect of this outside rein against the horse's neck is a pressure aid in its own right.

It is normal, and indeed important, for the indirect rein to aid our turns – across the diagonal, down the centre line, riding a square and so on. For example, turn left (as above) – left hand (unseen) gently opens and asks, right rein supports by moving indirectly against the neck. Circles and serpentines – indeed anything that concerns bending – require that the indirect rein allows but also supports the bend. The smaller the circle, the less the inside hand and the more the outside one plays an important role.

The only time the rein aids will tend to mimic each other is on a straight line: straight lines require both hands to mirror each other – with each rein just touching the horse's neck. Out hacking, we can often go for miles without thinking about our hands very much. In the school, the opposite scenario exists. As one rein asks or allows forward, the other regulates, then vice versa – more or less all the time. Thus, every time we see a corner or bend coming up, the new inside rein must be prepared to invite by asking and giving – with the younger horse, it will open. To complement this, the new outside rein should now offer support.

Every time we change the rein we should – without thinking – be changing the emphasis. What was the outside rein, acting on the outside of

In showjumping and eventing, the indirect rein is frequently used in the turns. Dressage riders may be less aware of its vital importance but its use is highly practical.

I have taught Prazer the levade as an advanced movement and this is very different from a rear. It requires great balance and strength in the horse's hocks and quarters. The weight of the rider is as close to the pommel as possible. The reins ideally should be soft or loose, depending on the horse.

the horse's body, becomes the inside. While its role is to invite or bend the horse into the opposite direction, the new outside rein will now support. It will clearly keep a check so that the horse remains on the track and moves ahead. None of this should involve any obvious movements and we may not even think about it consciously. From force of habit and general empathy, we learn to feel what works best for the horse.

Riding with the reins in one hand is a good way of understanding how the inside and outside rein affect the horse, and should be practised on a regular basis to improve the entire aiding process.

Harmonising the aids

I have already mentioned that, ideally, all aids will work in concert with each other at all times. Remember how sensitive the horse is. Be aware

that whatever you think, whatever you do, every small movement on your part involves a small weight change – even if unconsciously applied. Remember too that the word 'aid' means to help (indeed the Old Masters actually called them 'helpes') so we must help the horse with these subtle movements, not disturb his balance.

It is good to enjoy a long rein and stretch at the end of the session.

Once the horse can put his trust in the rider's hands, knowing they are there for him – simply to guide – never to punish and always to back up those other aids that we have been at pains to identify and explain, we should end up with a happy horse.

Happy horses make for happy riders. By being in balance with ourselves, we have a much better chance of being in balance with the horse. There will come a time when you only have to think right or left and somehow the horse knows.

For most of our forward riding, we should think of our two reins as being open to provide a clear, unfettered pathway for our horse to move ahead and through. Everyone has their own ideas about riding, but for me personally, visualisation plays an important part. With the energy of the horse moving forward from behind, the idea of a flowing river makes it much easier – quite unconsciously – to apply the correct rein, leg and weight aid at the same time.

For now, it is time to tune in to our natural instincts and ride naturally. There is no mystery to classical riding – the rules are all very simple but be prepared! It can take a lifetime to do well. Good luck! ■

In Conclusion

I hope this book will have made you more aware of the wonderful way in which horses and riders can work together without stress. Gentle discipline is important, but there should never be force in any partnership – or indeed at any time.

Instead, through study of riding, reading and watching, we can begin to visualise those hidden aids that nobody talks about. We can almost see the energy of the horse and feel the plumb line drop down through ourselves and the horse like a bolt from the blue – to connect us with gravity, upon which we both depend.

Prazer – my dearest friend – who reads me like a book.

Once we have felt those things and strive to work within Nature's Laws of balance and locomotion, everything becomes clearer. We can work out a logical plan and change things for the better and the result should herald a happier horse and a more confident rider.

Riding is all about 'feel', but without the theory of riding and without understanding the Laws of the Universe better, it is hard sometimes to accept the status quo.

What should help us more than anything is the way in which our horse reacts. If he seems muddled or confused, ask yourselves why. Were you not clear enough? Did you over-complicate your requests? Were you accurate with those requests? There is a fine line between asking for something natural and demanding something that is not.

Knowing how to balance and when and where to apply the aids should be simple, but it is very easy to allow our bodies to lie to us and to apply pressure where none was needed. Quite often we deter our horses by giving the very opposite of what they most need from us – the freedom to balance!

I don't believe you have to be a superb rider to get a superb reaction out of your horse. I believe all is possible through patience, giving the correct aids, and rewarding. Never get angry or impatient if your horse cannot change right away. Examine yourself and work out how you might do things in a manner that is easier for him. Think about letting go!

There is nearly always an answer to every conundrum and even if the work is not brilliant, be happy when you make it better. We should always praise frequently and generously – not just for the improvements, which will surely come – but for our horses having allowed us to ride them in the first place. There is insufficient awe in the attitudes of many riders. It is a pretty incredible thing that horses allow us to do all we do with them. Whatever the discipline, there has to be an amazing quantity of acceptance and trust on their part, and we don't always deserve it. Many people forget to thank their horse at the end of a lesson, and far more just take them for granted.

Like us, horses respond enormously to love and respect, and for those who have had a difficult start in life it is a real challenge and a privilege to turn their lives around. Neither should it matter how long it takes.

For me, the discipline of riding is to know yourself as well as your horse. Through their generosity, our lives can be transformed and, from every pony or horse in your life, something will have been learned. To me, they are God's own creatures and I never cease to wonder at their beauty, generosity and spirit. Once you acknowledge that you will never be quite the same again. All I can say to them is 'thank you'! ∎

Prazer and I enjoying our flowers (in our own separate ways) at the end of another Lusitano Breed Show.

Acknowledgements

This book has always been about the photographs. I am indebted to Quiller, my Publishers, who liked the idea as horses are so naturally photogenic. It was clear from the start that twenty or thirty words of caption for each and every picture could supplant reams of prosy explanation.

It has therefore been a joy to work with some wonderful horses, students and friends. Most of all, my Lusitano stallion Prazer – or Mr P as he is affectionately known – was clearly determined to make this last book possible. As a young five year old, he was totally inspirational and a delight to bring on, eventually turning into my best schoolmaster ever. It seems more than coincidence that his registered name in the Portuguese Stud Book translates as 'pleasure'.

Instruction by photographs is not a new discipline and visual teaching is very powerful. In the case of rider position and the application of the aids, there is nothing quite like it. Even videos do not capture the moment so strongly. Still – as opposed to moving – pictures definitely allow us that missing ingredient. They give us time for observation and contemplation. For this reason, it has been very special putting this book together.

None of this might have happened had I not met photographer Anthony Osmond-Evans who is also the publisher of many beautiful photographic books. These include the much acclaimed *The Spirit of London*, published in celebration of the 2012 London Olympic Games which also coincided with Her Majesty the Queen's Diamond Jubilee. Each Olympiad, from all over the world, was presented with a copy of Anthony's stunning oeuvre by the Mayor of London, Boris Johnson.

You do not of course have to be an Olympic contender to own my latest book. I am privileged that Anthony has taken the bulk of all the amazing photographs for *The Rider's Balance*. Very quickly, he understood the essence of what I wanted to show my readers – and although he is not a horseman himself – he has great empathy for all horses. He has worked tirelessly to help me bring this book to fruition and the standard of his work and effort put in has been overwhelming.

By taking time to study these pictures and their relevant captions, you will be able to train your eye to appreciate the different applications of weight in each and every movement. These were by no means set up just for this book. They clearly happen for real during training and show us why each small adjustment to our weight works so admirably for the horse. It is subtle and totally natural.

I have many friends within the horse world who have been involved. As well as Anthony, I am so grateful to photographers Risto Aaltonen, Black Tent Publications, Kristine Wilson, Nathalie Todd, Tina Layton-Elliott, Tino Fernandez, Andrew Carter and Susan Young. Particular mention should be made of the kind help photographer Peter Draper has also given me behind the scenes.

I would also like to thank all the owners who allowed us to use their immaculate yards for our various photo-shoots. Gail Adams has been particularly generous in this way. Finally, I am indebted to all the guest riders and their horses – what could we have done without you?

In no particular order they include Jen Sims, Robert Smith QC, Alice Cornwell, Lucy Haycock, Catherine Saphire Dachtler, Helen Trivette, Deborah Bone, Becky Cheeseman, Ali Formstone, Karen Coulbeck, Pamela Harley, John Tanner, Alexandra Downing, Julianne Fernandez, Francisco de Bragança and Vicky Slack. Amongst these, a special word of thanks must go to my good friend Tina Layton-Elliott who owns the Contessa Riding Centre in Hertfordshire. She and her son, Zak Layton-Elliott, Wanda Bendisch, Emma Slater and Leila Khaldi are also represented in these pages.

I must just mention a few special people who have gone out of their way to be supportive of this my last equestrian book. What would one do without this sort of loyalty? They include Sarah Philpott, Sue Durkan, Anne Wilson, Abigail Burns, Lesley Sendall and my ever-encouraging daughter, Allegra Loch.

Finally, a warm word of thanks must go to Liz Storey who has worked tirelessly in this office for the last several months of completing this book. I am hopeless at moving photographs and text about on the computer and she has held my hand throughout and been wonderful about prompting me to do this or that and organising my worktop and dining-room table. The latter has been littered with over 2,500 small stamp-sized photographs for the past several months and somehow she has helped me find the relevant pictures and quietly popped them into my chosen location in the correct order and chapter. Not an easy task while I swayed between – 'will it go here?'... or 'should it go there?' She has been an absolute treasure.

This has been my most challenging book to date, not just because the subject is so complex but because I am not as young as I was! It is not easy being close to an author and I must thank all those who are nearest and dearest for putting up with me so gallantly.

Thank you as ever to my wise and painstaking editor Martin Diggle and to Maggie Raynor, whose excellent drawings many of you will know. I would especially like to thank all my readers for your patience and particularly those who have supported me over so many years through The Classical Riding Club and our very lively Facebook page. That really has helped to keep me going – as of course have the horses – as always.

Finally, a huge thank you to Charlotte Dujardin for her most generous Foreword and to Carl Hester who never fails to make time to help others. He, together with his assistant Claudine Bichard, have been absolutely brilliant and I am so grateful for all their kind efforts.

As for the horses – all I can say is God bless them all!

Sylvia Loch